KU-443-660

# EASY TOYS TO CROCHET

## Dolls, animals and gifts for children

LIBRARIES NI
WITHDRAWN FROM STOCK

## Claire Garland

PAVILION

First published in the United Kingdom in 2015 by
Pavilion Books Company Limited
1 Gower Street
London
WC1E 6HD

Copyright © Pavilion Books 2015

All rights reserved. No part of this publication may be copied,
displayed, extracted, reproduced, utilised, stored in a retrieval system
or transmitted in any form or by any means, electronic, mechanical
or otherwise including but not limited to photocopying, recording, or
scanning without the prior written permission of the publishers. The
patterns contained in this book and the items created from them are for
personal use only. Commercial use of either the patterns or items made
from them is strictly prohibited.

ISBN 978-1-90981-595-7

A CIP catalogue record for this book is available
from the British Library.

10 9 8 7 6 5 4 3 2 1

Reproduction by Mission, Hong Kong
Printed and bound by 1010 Printing International Ltd, China

This book can be ordered direct from the publisher at
www.pavilionbooks.com

# Contents

# Introduction

I've always found crochet to be a craft of myriad benefits. On a professional level, it is a design tool that provides ease and workability – what other craft allows you to create perfect circles in a matter of a few simple knots? On a personal note, crocheting is a stress-reliever and an ideal way to unwind after a long day. With just a hook and a ball of yarn, crocheting offers an immediate sense of accomplishment and release, especially when making toys.

My creative inspiration for these projects was sparked by my children: I love the way they create miniature worlds and how their toys develop into loveable friends and cuddly beasts. My objective in this book was to devise a collection of unique and character-driven toys. The results, I hope, are fun creations that are totally endearing.

I couldn't choose a favourite from among the projects – they all brim with personality, and I adore them equally. The Mermaid, with her cascading mane and long, crocheted fin, radiates beauty; the Giraffe, with her jolly scarf and dress, is a stylish creature; and Sir Waldorf Walrus is a grand old gentleman of the seas.

All the projects in this book are simple to make and require very little time to finish, which is great if you have an anxious child peering over your shoulder. (I recommend stitching up a couple of finger puppets for such an occasion!) I hope the projects in this book bring as much satisfaction to you as they did for me. I thoroughly enjoyed designing and making each toy, and I hope I have expressed this pleasure on every page.

Enjoy and get hooked!

# Crochet Basics

This book is not aimed at complete beginners, although many of the projects are simple enough to tackle without much experience, and I hope they will inspire you to move on to some of the more complex toys. Below are a few useful points to bear in mind.

## UK and US crochet terms

In the patterns, we give UK crochet stitch names first, with the US equivalents following, separated by a slash. If you find this confusing to follow, try photocopying the patterns you would like to make and highlighting instructions in the 'language' you are most familiar with. Below are some of the key differences:

### UK terms and US conversions

double crochet (dc) = single crochet (sc)
half treble (htr) = half double crochet (hdc)
treble (tr) = double crochet (dc)
double treble (dtr) = treble (tr)

## Abbreviations

**beg** beginning
**ch** chain(s)
**ch sp** chain space(s)
**cm** centimetre(s)
**cont** continue
**dc** double crochet (NB: both UK and US term)
**dc2tog** double crochet two stitches together
**dc3tog** double crochet three stitches together
**dec** decrease
**dtr** double treble (NB: UK term only)
**foll** following
**hdc** half double crochet (NB: US term only)
**htr** half treble crochet (NB: UK term only)
**in** inch(es)
**inc** increase
**m** metre(s)
**mm** millimetre(s)
**rem** remaining
**rep** repeat
**RS** right side

**sc** single crochet (NB: US term only)
**sl st** slip st
**sp** space(s)
**st(s)** stitch(es)
**tch** turning chain
**tog** together
**tr** treble (NB: both UK and US term)
**WS** wrong side
**yd** yard(s)
**[ ]** work instructions in square brackets as directed

## Yarns

Many of the projects are quite small-scale and will not require a full ball of yarn to complete, so you can take this opportunity to do some stash-busting! Many of the yarns are readily convertible to whatever you have to hand, so do not feel you need to stick rigidly to the recommended yarns. As long as you follow the suggested yarn weight, and of course keep to the tension (gauge) set out in the pattern instructions, most yarns will be suitable, whether they are pure wool, wool blends, acrylic, cotton or other blends. The only exception is where the project suggests using a textured or fluffy yarn – Jenna the Giraffe's scarf, for example (page 81), uses a fluffy yarn for effect.

## Hook conversions

You should be aware that different parts of the crocheting world use different sizing systems for crochet hooks. In this book we list both metric sizes (the measurement is in millimetres) and US sizes – the US has its own idiosyncratic sizing system.

| Metric | US |
|--------|------|
| 2.50 | – |
| 2.75 | C-2 |
| 3.00 | – |
| 3.25 | D-3 |
| 3.50 | E-4 |
| 3.75 | F-5 |
| 4.00 | 6 |
| 4.50 | 7 |
| 5.00 | H-8 |
| 5.50 | I-9 |
| 6.00 | J-10 |
| 6.50 | K10½ |
| 7.00 | 11 |
| 8.00 | L-12 |
| 9.00 | M-13 |
| 10.00 | N-15 |

behind the point at which the thread came out. Bring the needle out about 3mm (⅛in) in front of the starting point. Continue in the same manner.

## French knot

Bring the needle out on the surface of the fabric at the place where the knot is to lie. Wrap the thread around the needle two or three times, depending on how big you want the knot to be. Insert the needle close to where it came out. Holding the knot in place, pull the needle to the wrong side to secure the knot.

## Oversew

Sew the two edges together with close stitches that pass over them both approximately 3mm (⅛in) from the edge of both edges.

## Satin stitch

Work parallel straight stitches, close together, across the entire area of a shape to fill it.

## Techniques for finishing touches

Here are some useful sewing and embroidery stitches that are used to add finishing touches to the toys.

## Backstitch

Use for sewing strong seams or for attaching trims by hand. Bring the needle up from the underside of the fabric and insert it about 3mm (⅛in)

## Stem stitch

Bring the needle to the front at the left-hand side of the working line. With the thread beneath the needle, take it through to the back just beneath the working line. Pull the needle through. The thread at this point creates a very slight diagonal to the working line. Continue making these diagonal stitches along the working line, keeping all the stitches the same size.

# Dolls and Dolls' Clothes

This chapter contains patterns for a doll, a basic bear with a variety of clothes, and several adorable accessories. Once you have conquered the basics, take your pick from this collection of loveable projects and make a mermaid, a sailor or a hula hula dancer.

# Basic Bear

**This classic bear can be crocheted up without a hitch. Use him as the foundation for Sailor Bear (page 40), or combine him with other basic clothes (page 26) to create your own unique teddy.**

## SIZE
31cm (12¼in) tall x 35cm (13¾in) wide (arms outstretched)

## MATERIALS
One 50g ball of aran-weight (worsted) wool yarn in cream for bear (MC)
Black embroidery thread for mouth and for attaching beads
Two 6mm (¼in) black glass pearls or similar for eyes
Dark blue embroidery thread for nose
5.00mm (H-8) crochet hook
Polyester toy stuffing or wadding
Yarn needle

## TENSION (GAUGE)
9 sts and 8 rnds to 5cm (2in) over dc/sc.

## NOTE
Before beginning the second round in each section, place a marker or short length of contrasting yarn across your crochet and up against the loop on the hook and above the working yarn. Work Rnd 2, then slip the marker out and place it at the beginning of the next round and so on. The marker will indicate where each subsequent round starts.

## HEAD
**Foundation row:** Beg at the nose end and using MC, make 2ch.
**Rnd 1:** 8dc/8sc in 2nd ch from hook.
**Rnd 2:** [1dc/1sc in each of next 2dc/2sc, 2dc/2sc in next dc/sc] twice, 1dc/1sc in each of next 2dc/2sc (10dc/10sc).
**Rnd 3:** 1dc/1sc in each dc/sc around.
**Shape top of nose:**
**Rnd 4:** [1dc/1sc in each of next 2dc/2sc, 2dc/2sc in next dc/sc) 3 times, 1dc/sc in next dc/sc (13dc/13sc).
**Rnd 5:** 1dc/1sc in each dc/sc around.
**Rnd 6:** *2dc/2sc in each dc/sc around (26dc/26sc).
**Rnd 7:** 1dc/1sc in each dc/sc around.

**Rnd 8:** [1dc/1sc in each of next 3dc/3sc, 2dc/2sc in next dc/sc] 5 times, 1dc/1sc in next 6dc/6sc (31dc/21sc).

**Rnd 9:** 1dc/1sc in each dc/sc around.

**Shape back of head:**

**Rnd 10:** Miss first dc/sc, *1dc/1sc in each of next 4dc/4sc, miss next dc/sc, rep from * to end (24dc/24sc).

**Rnd 11:** 1dc/1sc in each dc/sc around.

**Rnd 12**: *1dc/1sc in each of next 3dc/3sc, miss next dc/sc, rep from * to end (18dc/18sc).

**Rnd 13:** *1dc/1sc in each of next 2dc/2sc, miss next dc/sc, rep from * to end (12dc/12sc).

Turn out to RS. Stuff the head lightly.

**Rnd 14:** *1dc/1sc in next dc/sc, miss next dc/sc, rep from * to end (6dc/6sc).

Rep last row until gap is closed.

Fasten off. Weave in ends.

**EARS (make 2)**

**Foundation row:** Beg at the ear base and using MC, make 2ch.

**Row 1:** 6dc/6sc in 2nd ch from hook, turn.

**Row 2:** 1ch, 1dc/1sc in top half of each dc/sc along. Fasten off, leaving a tail end long enough to handsew the ears onto the head.

**BODY**

**Foundation row:** Beg at the bottom and using MC, make 4ch, join with sl st at the top of first ch to make a ring.

**Rnd 1:** 12htr/12hdc in ring.

**Rnd 2:** 1htr/1hdc in each htr/hdc around.

**Rnd 3:** *1htr/1hdc in next htr/hdc, 2htr/2hdc in next htr/hdc, rep from * to end (18htr/18hdc).

**Rnd 4:** 1htr/1hdc in each htr/hdc around. Rep last 2 rnds once more (27htr/27hdc).

**Rnd 7:** 1htr/1hdc in each htr/hdc around.

**Shape back:**

**Rnd 8:** [1htr/1hdc in next htr/hdc, miss next htr/hdc] 5 times, 1htr/1hdc in each of next 17htr/17hdc (22htr/22hdc).

**Rnd 9:** [1htr/1hdc in next htr/hdc, miss next htr/hdc) 4 times, 1htr/1hdc in each of next 11htr/11hdc (18htr/18hdc).

**Rnd 10:** 1htr/1hdc in each htr/hdc around.

Rep last rnd once more.

**Rnd 12:** *1htr/1hdc in next htr/hdc, miss next htr/hdc, rep from * to end (9htr/9hdc).

Stuff the body.

**Rnd 13:** *1htr/1hdc in each of next 2htr/2hdc, miss next htr/hdc, rep from * to end (6htr/6hdc).

Fasten off, leaving a tail end long enough to join the body to the head.

## ARMS (make 2)

**Foundation row (RS):** Beg at the top of the arm and using MC, make 21ch.

**Row 1 (WS):** 1dc/1sc in 2nd ch from hook, 1dc/1sc in each ch to end, turn (20dc/20sc).

**Row 2 (RS):** 1ch, 1dc/1sc in each dc/sc to end, turn (20dc/20sc).

Rep last row 3 times more.

### Shape hand:

**Row 6 (RS):** 1ch, 1dc/1sc in each of next 6dc/6sc, turn.

**Row 7 (WS):** 1ch, miss next dc/sc, 1dc/1sc in each dc/sc across, turn (5dc/5sc).

**Row 8 (RS):** 1ch, miss next dc/sc, 1dc/1sc in each dc/sc across, turn (4dc/4sc).

**Row 9 (WS):** 1ch, miss next dc/sc, 1dc/1sc in next dc/sc, miss next dc/sc, 1dc/1sc in next dc/sc (3dc/3sc).

Fasten off, leaving a tail end long enough for you to sew the arm seam.

### Join other half of hand:

With RS facing and working along foundation row edge, count in 6ch from hand end, pull though yarn MC to 6th ch, 1ch, 1dc/1sc in each ch to end (6dc/6sc).

**Row 2 (WS):** 1ch, miss next dc/sc, 1dc/1sc in each dc/sc across, turn (5dc/5sc).

**Row 3 (RS):** 1ch, miss next dc/sc, 1dc/1sc in each dc/sc across, turn (4dc/4sc).

**Row 4 (WS):** 1ch, miss next dc/sc, 1dc/1sc in next dc/sc, miss next dc/sc, 1dc/1sc in next dc/sc (2dc/2sc).

Fasten off.

## LEGS (make 2)

**Foundation row:** Beg at toe and using MC, make 2ch.

**Rnd 1:** 6dc/6sc in 2nd ch from hook.

**Rnd 2:** *1dc/1sc in next dc/sc, 2dc/2sc in next dc/sc, rep from * around (9dc/9sc).

**Rnd 3:** 1dc/1sc in each dc/sc around.

Rep last rnd 5 times more.

### Shape heel:

**Row 9:** 1dc/1sc in each of next 4dc/4sc, turn.

**Row 10:** 1ch, 1dc/1sc in each of next 4dc/4sc, turn.

Rep last row once more.

Fasten off. Join heel seam – fold the finishing row (last 4dc/4sc) in half so that the two ends meet and sew together to form back of heel.

### Shape top of foot:

**Rnd 1:** Join in yarn MC with a sl st at top of heel seam, work 4dc/4sc along first row-end edge of heel, 1dc/1sc in each

of 5dc/5sc across front of foot, then 4dc/4sc along 2nd row-end edge of heel (13dc/13sc).

**Rnd 2:** 1dc/1sc in each of next 13dc/13sc.

**Shape ankle:**

**Rnd 3:** [1dc/1sc in each of next 3dc/3sc, miss next dc/sc] 3 times, 1dc/1sc in next dc/sc (10dc/10sc).

**Rnd 4:** 1dc/1sc in each of next 10dc/10sc.

Rep last rnd until the leg measures 19cm (7½in) from toe.

Fasten off.

## TO FINISH

Referring to the photograph for the positioning of eyes, handsew a bead on either side of the nose.

Using dark blue embroidery thread, handsew the nose with a few horizontal stitches.

Sew a mouth using six strands of black embroidery thread by securing a length of thread at the corner of the mouth position at the back of the face, bring the thread to the front, reinserting at the length you want the mouth to be. Sew a short stitch in the middle of the stitched line, securing the stitch down.

Stuff the body fairly firmly. Close the gap at the bottom. Handsew the head to the body. Oversew the arms to join, stuffing the hands lightly. Stuff the feet. Sew the arms to the side of the body and the legs to the bottom. Sew the ears to the top of the head.

If you wish, you can handsew a button (10mm/⅜in in diameter) to the back of the bear's waist. This will help to hold up the trousers or skirt (see Basic Clothes, page 26) if you choose to make them for the bear. The button needs to be small enough to go through a dc/sc stitch, yet large enough to secure the garments.

# Basic Doll

**This pattern is the foundation for Hula Hula Lula (page 36) and Molly the Mermaid (page 46). Make a stylish ensemble for the doll from the Basic Clothes (page 26).**

## SIZE
42cm (16½in) tall x 50cm (19¾in) wide (arms outstretched)

## MATERIALS
One 50g ball of DK-weight (light worsted) wool and alpaca blend in beige or other suitable flesh colour for doll's body (MC)
One 50g ball of DK-weight (light worsted) yarn in hair colour of your choice (or use a mix of colours as we have) (A)
Small amount of DK-weight (light worsted) wool or wool blend yarn in pale blue for tankini (B)
3.50mm (E-4) and 4.00mm (G-6) hooks
Small pieces of felt for eyes
Black thread for sewing on eyes
Two 6mm (¼in) black glass beads or similar for eyes
Pink embroidery thread for sewing mouth
Polyester toy stuffing or wadding
Yarn needle

## TENSION (GAUGE)
**For doll:** 12 sts and 12 rnds to 5cm (2in) using 3.50mm (E-4) hook and yarn MC over dc/sc.

**For tankini:** 9 sts and 10 rows to 5cm (2in) using 4.00mm (G-6) hook and yarn B over dc/sc.

## NOTE
Before beginning the second round in each section, place a marker or short length of contrasting yarn across your crochet and up against the loop on the hook and above the working yarn. Work Rnd 2 then slip the marker out and place it at the beginning of the next round and so on. The marker will indicate where each subsequent round starts.

# Doll

## HEAD & BODY
Make back and front alike.
**Foundation row:** Using yarn MC and 3.50mm (E-4) hook, beg at the base, make 13ch.
**Row 1:** 1dc/1sc in 2nd ch from hook, 1dc/1sc in each ch across, turn (12dc/12sc).
**Row 2:** 2ch, 1dc/1sc in 2nd ch from hook, 1dc/1sc in each dc/sc to last dc/sc, 2dc/2sc in last dc/sc, turn (14dc/14sc).
**Row 3:** 1ch, 1dc/1sc in each dc/sc across, turn.
Rep last 2 rows twice more (18dc/18sc).
**Row 8:** 1ch, 1dc/1sc in each of next 18dc/18sc, turn (18dc/18sc).
Rep last row 8 times more.
### Shape body and neck:
**Row 17:** 1ch, miss first dc/sc, 1dc/1sc in each dc/sc to last 2dc/2sc, miss next dc/sc, 1dc/sc in last dc/sc, turn (16dc/16sc).
Rep last row 3 times more (10dc/10sc).
**Row 21:** 1ch, 1dc/1sc in each dc/sc across, turn (10dc/10sc).
Rep last row 5 times more.
### Shape head:
**Row 27:** 2ch, 1dc/1sc in 2nd ch from hook, 1dc/1sc in each dc/sc to last dc/sc, 2dc/2sc in last dc/sc, turn (12dc/12sc).

Rep last row twice more (16dc/16sc).
**Row 30:** 1ch, 1dc/1sc in each dc/sc across, turn (16dc/16sc).
Rep last row 3 times more.
### Shape top of head:
**Row 34:** 1ch, miss first dc/sc, 1dc/1sc in each dc/sc to last 2dc/2sc, miss next dc/sc, 1dc/1sc in last dc/sc, turn (14dc/14sc).
Rep last row 4 times more (6dc/6sc).
Fasten off.

## ARMS (make 2)
**Foundation row:** Using yarn MC and 3.50mm (E-4) hook, make 38ch.
**Row 1:** 1dc/1sc in 2nd ch from hook, 1dc/1sc in each ch across, turn (37dc/37sc).
**Row 2:** 1ch, 1dc/1sc in each dc/sc across, turn (37dc/37sc).
Rep last row twice more.
Fasten off, leaving a long tail end – use this to oversew along the foundation and finishing rows to join.

## FEET & LEGS (make 2)
**Foundation row:** Using yarn MC and 3.50mm (E-4) hook, beg at toe, make 2ch.
**Rnd 1:** 6dc/6sc in 2nd ch from hook.
**Rnd 2:** *1dc/1sc in next dc/sc, 2dc/2sc in next dc/sc, rep from * around (9dc/9sc).
**Rnd 3:** 1dc/1sc in each of next 9dc/9sc.

Rep last rnd 5 times more.

**Shape heel:**

**Row 1:** 1dc/1sc in each of next 4dc/4sc, turn.

**Row 2:** 1ch, 1dc/1sc in each of next 4dc/4sc, turn.

Rep last row once more.

Fasten off. Join heel seam – fold the finishing row (last 4dc/4sc) in half so that the two ends meet and sew together to form back of heel.

**Shape top of foot:**

**Rnd 1:** Join in yarn MC with a sl st at top of heel seam, work 4dc/4sc along first row-end edge of heel, 1dc/1sc in each of 5dc/5sc across front of foot, then 4dc/4sc along second row-end edge of heel (13dc/13sc).

**Rnd 2:** 1dc/1sc in each of next 13dc/13sc.

**Shape ankle:**

**Rnd 3:** [1dc/1sc in each of next 3dc/3sc, miss next dc/sc] 3 times, 1dc/1sc in last dc/sc, turn (10dc/10sc).

Stuff the foot.

**Rnd 4:** 1dc/1sc in each of next 10dc/10sc.

Rep last rnd until the leg measures 23cm (9in) from toe.

Fasten off.

**TO FINISH**

Cut out two circles from felt 10mm (³⁄₈in)

in diameter for the irises. Sew a bead to the centre of each iris. Referring to the photograph for positioning, sew the eyes to the face.

Sew a mouth using six strands of pink embroidery thread by securing a length of yarn at the corner of the mouth position at the back of the face. Bring the yarn to the front and reinsert at the desired mouth length. Sew a short stitch in the middle of the stitched line, securing the stitch down a little to form the bottom lip. Work another stitch above this 'caught' stitch to form the upper lip.

Using a blunt-ended yarn needle and yarn MC, join the front of the body to the back, leaving the bottom edge open for stuffing. Stuff the doll firmly in the head, and very lightly in the trunk. Close the gap at the bottom.

Oversew the arms to join. Sew the arms to the side of the body. Sew the legs to the bottom of the body.

To sew on the hair, cut yarn A into lengths of 36cm (14¼in). Taking one length at a time, bend it in half and, using a crochet hook, pull the loop through a dc/sc stitch at the top of the head, referring to the photograph for hair placement. Pass the cut ends through the loops, then pull the cut ends firmly so that the knot lies at the top of the head. Continue with this fringing technique along the top and a little way

down the back of the head, depending on how thick you want the hair to be.

# Tankini

## BOTTOM

**Foundation row:** Using yarn B and 4.00mm (G-6) hook, make 33ch.
**Row 1:** 1dc/1sc in 2nd ch from hook, 1dc/1sc in each ch across, turn (32dc/32sc).
**Row 2:** 1ch, 1dc/1sc in each of next 32dc/32sc, join into ring with sl st in first dc/sc, taking care not to twist the rows (32dc/32sc).
Cont to work in rnds.
**Rnd 1:** 1dc/1sc in each dc/sc around (32dc/32sc).
Rep last rnd twice more.
**Shape front:**
**Row 1:** 1dc/1sc in each of next 12dc/12sc, turn (12dc/12sc).
**Row 2:** 1ch, 1dc/1sc in each of next 12dc/12sc, turn.
**Row 3:** 1ch, miss first dc/sc, 1dc/1sc in each of next 9dc/9sc, miss next dc/sc, 1dc/1sc in last dc/sc, turn (10dc/10sc).
**Row 4:** 1ch, 1dc/1sc in each of next 10dc/10sc, turn (10dc/10sc).
**Row 5:** 1ch, miss first dc/sc, 1dc/1sc in

each of next 7dc/7sc, miss next dc/sc, 1dc/1sc in last dc/sc, turn (8dc/8sc).
**Row 6:** 1ch, 1dc/1sc in each of next 8dc/8sc, turn (8dc/8sc).
**Row 7:** 1ch, miss first dc/sc, 1dc/1sc in each of next 5dc/5sc, miss next dc/sc, 1dc/1sc in last dc/sc, turn (6dc/6sc).
**Row 8:** 1ch, 1dc/1sc in each of next 6dc/6sc, turn (6dc/6sc).
**Row 9:** 1ch, miss first dc/sc, 1dc/1sc in each of next 3dc/3sc, miss next dc/sc, 1dc/1sc in last dc/sc, turn (4dc/4sc).
**Row 10:** 1ch, 1dc/1sc in each of next 4dc/4sc (4dc/4sc).
Fasten off, leaving a long tail end for sewing up the gusset seam.
**Shape back:**
**Row 1:** With RS facing, join in yarn B to first of 20 rem dc/sc at left back, 1ch, miss dc/sc where yarn was joined, 1dc/1sc in each of next 17dc/17sc, miss next dc/sc, 1dc/1sc in last dc/sc, turn (18dc/18sc).
**Row 2:** 1ch, miss first dc/sc, 1dc/1sc in each to last dc/sc, miss last dc/sc, turn (16dc/16sc).
Rep last row 6 times more, turn (4dc/4sc).
**Row 9:** 1ch, 1dc/1sc in each of next 4dc/4sc.
Fasten off, weave in loose end.

## TO FINISH
With RS facing and matching yarn, sew up the short waist seam and gusset seam, leaving the legs open.

## TOP
**Foundation row:** Using yarn B and 4.00mm (G-6) hook, make 18ch, turn.
**Row 1:** 1dc/1sc in 2nd ch from hook, 1dc/1sc in each ch across, turn (17dc/17sc).
**Row 2:** 1ch, 1dc/1sc in each of next 17dc/17sc, turn.
**Row 3:** 1ch, 1 dc/1sc in first dc/sc, *miss 1dc/1sc, 5tr/5dc in next dc/sc, miss 1dc/1sc, 1dc/1sc in next dc/sc, rep from * to end.
Fasten off.
For the back strap, make a chain long enough to fit across the back and sew to row ends of the top.
For each shoulder strap, make a chain long enough to fit over the shoulders. Sew one end of each strap to the foundation row of the top and the other end to the back strap.

## Note
See page 32 to make the doll's shoes.

# Basic Clothes

A fashionable girl-about-town needs a chic urban wardrobe to reflect her unique personality. Many of these garments are the basics for other clothes within this chapter. A hat and striped culottes look fabulous day and night, while a button-up hoodie is ideal outerwear when the temperature drops.

## Hooded cardigan

### SIZE
20 x 24cm (8 x 9½in) from bottom to tip of hood

### MATERIALS
One 50g ball of DK-weight (light worsted) acrylic and nylon blend in lilac (MC)
Small amount of DK-weight (light worsted) wool or wool blend in damson (A)
5.00mm (H-8) hook
Three 18mm (¾in) buttons
Yarn needle

### TENSION (GAUGE)
9 sts and 7 rows to 5cm (2in) using yarn MC over dc/sc.

### NOTE
Before beginning the second round in each section, place a marker or short length of contrasting yarn across your crochet and up against the loop on the hook and above the working yarn. Work Rnd 2 then slip the marker out and place it at the beginning of the next round and so on. The marker will indicate where each subsequent round starts.

### FRONT
**Foundation row:** Beg at right centre front, and using yarn A, make 12ch.
**Row 1 (RS):** 2dc/2sc in 2nd ch from hook, 1dc/1sc in each ch across, turn (12dc/12sc).
**Row 2:** 1ch, 1dc/1sc in first dc/sc, (miss next 2dc/2sc, make buttonhole by making 2ch, 1dc/1sc in each of next 2dc/2sc) twice, miss next 2dc/2sc, make 2ch, 2dc/2sc in last dc/sc, turn (13 sts).
**Row 3:** Join in yarn MC with a sl st in last dc/sc of previous row, 1ch, 2dc/2sc in first dc/sc, 1dc/1sc in next dc/sc,

2dc/2sc in next 2ch sp, (1dc/1sc in each of next 2dc/2sc, 2dc/2sc in next 2ch sp) twice, 1dc/1sc in last dc/sc, turn (14dc/14sc).

**Row 4:** 1ch, 1dc/1sc in each dc/sc across, turn.

**Row 5:** 1ch, 2dc/2sc in first dc/sc, 1dc/1sc in each dc/sc across, turn (15dc/15sc).

**Row 6:** 1ch, 1dc/1sc in each dc/sc across, turn.

Rep last row 3 times more.

**Make right armhole:**

**Row 10 (WS):** 1ch, 1dc/1sc in each of next 6dc/6sc, miss next 7dc/7sc, make 7ch, 1dc/1sc in each of next 2dc/2sc, turn.

**Make back:**

**Row 11 (RS):** 1ch, 1dc/1sc in each of next 2dc/2sc, 1dc/1sc in each of next 7ch, 1dc/1sc in each of next 6dc/6sc, turn.

**Row 12:** 1ch, 1dc/1sc in each dc/sc across, turn.

Rep last row 8 times more.

**Make left armhole:**

**Row 21 (RS):** 1ch, 1dc/1sc in each of next 2dc/2sc, miss next 7dc/7sc, make 7ch, 1dc/1sc in each of next 6dc/6sc, turn.

**Row 22:** 1ch, 1dc/1sc in each of next 6dc/6sc, 1dc/1sc in each of next 7ch, 1dc/1sc in each of next 2dc/2sc, turn (15dc/15sc).

**Row 23:** 1ch, 1dc/1sc in each dc/sc across, turn.

Rep last row 3 times more.

**Row 27 (RS):** Sl st in first dc/sc, 1ch, 1dc/1sc in each dc/sc across, turn (14dc/14sc).

**Row 28:** 1ch, 1dc/1sc in each dc/sc to last dc/sc, miss last dc/sc, turn (13dc/13sc).

Rep last 2 rows once more.

**Row 31 (RS):** Sl st in first dc/sc, 1ch, 1dc/1sc in each dc/sc across (10dc/10sc). Fasten off.

## SLEEVES (make 2)

**Rnd 1:** With RS facing, join yarn MC with a sl st into a dc/sc at base of armhole and drawing a loop through, make 1ch, 1dc/1sc in each dc/sc along edges of armhole, join with sl st in top of first dc/sc, turn (14dc/14sc).

**Rnd 2:** Working from the inside of the cardigan, 1ch, 1dc/1sc in each of next 14dc/14sc.

Rep last rnd until the entire sleeve – from Rnd 1 – measures 8cm (3in), ending with a sl st in top of first dc/sc. Fasten off and weave in ends.

## HOOD

**Row 1:** With RS facing, join on MC with a sl st into the dc/sc at beg of right centre front and, drawing a loop

through, make 1ch, work 30dc/30sc along neck edge to left centre front, turn.

**Row 2:** Sl st in first dc/sc, 1ch, 1dc/1sc in each of next 27dc/27sc, miss next dc/sc, 1dc/1sc in last dc/sc, turn (28dc/28sc).

**Row 3:** 1ch, 1dc/1sc in each dc/sc across, turn.

**Row 4:** Sl st in first dc/sc, 1ch, 1dc/1sc in each of next 25dc/25sc, miss next dc/sc, 1dc/1sc in last dc/sc, turn (26dc/26sc).

**Row 5:** 1ch, 1dc/1sc in each dc/sc across, turn.

**Row 6:** Sl st in first dc/sc, 1ch, 1dc/1sc in each of next 23dc/23sc, miss next dc/sc, 1dc/1sc in last dc/sc, turn (24dc/24sc).

**Row 7:** 1ch, 1dc/1sc in each dc/sc across, turn.

Rep last row 4 times more.

**Row 12:** 1ch, 1dc/1sc in each of next 11dc/11sc, [2dc/2sc in next dc/sc] twice, 1dc/1sc in each of next 11dc/11sc, turn (26dc/26sc).

**Row 13:** 1ch, 1dc/1sc in each dc/sc across, turn.

**Row 14:** 1ch, 1dc/1sc in each of next 12dc/12sc, [2dc/2sc in next dc/sc] twice, 1dc/1sc in each of next 12dc/12sc, turn (28dc/28sc).

**Row 15:** 1ch, 1dc/1sc in each dc/sc across, turn.

**Row 16:** 1ch, 1dc/1sc in each of next 13dc/13sc, [2dc/2sc in next dc/sc] twice, 1dc/1sc in each of next 13dc/13sc, turn (30dc/30sc).

**Row 17:** 1ch, 1dc/1sc in each dc/sc across, turn.

**Row 18:** 1ch, 1dc/1sc in each of next 14dc/14sc, [2dc/2sc in next dc/sc] twice, 1dc/1sc in each of next 14dc/14sc, turn (32dc/32sc).

**Row 19:** 1ch, 1dc/1sc in each dc/sc across. Fasten off, leaving a tail end long enough to sew up the seam with. With RS facing, sew up the hood along the finishing row.

Weave in end.

## HOOD EDGING

With RS facing, join in yarn A with a sl st into the last dc/sc worked at end of button band and, drawing a loop through, make 1ch, 1dc/1sc in each row-end edge along hood edge to left centre front, ending in sl st in top of last dc/sc. Fasten off.

# Basic trousers

## SIZE

17cm (6¾in) long x 23cm (9in) in diameter around waist

## MATERIALS

One 50g ball of DK-weight (light worsted) alpaca and wool blend in grey-blue (MC)

One 50g ball of DK-weight (light worsted) alpaca and wool blend in cream (A)

5.00mm (H-8) hook

30cm (12in) length of 6mm (¼in) ribbon

## TENSION (GAUGE)

8 sts and 9 rows to 5cm (2in) using yarn MC over dc/sc.

## TROUSERS

Follow this colour sequence throughout the pattern:

**Foundation row and Row 1:** Yarn MC.

**Rows 2 and 3:** Yarn A.

**Rows 4 and 5:** Yarn MC.

**Rows 6 and 7:** Yarn A, and so on.

**Foundation row:** Using yarn MC, beg at the leg end, make 27ch.

**Row 1:** 1dc/1sc in 2nd ch from hook, 1dc/1sc in each ch across, turn (26dc/26sc).

**Row 2:** 1ch, 1dc/1sc in each dc/sc across, turn.

Rep last row once more.

**Row 4:** 1ch, 1dc/1sc in each dc/sc across, turn, join into a ring with a sl st in first dc/sc of row, taking care not to twist the rows. Cont to work in rnds as follows:

**Rnd 1:** 1ch, 1dc/1sc in each of next 26dc/26sc around, join with a sl st in first dc/sc of row (26dc/26sc).

**Rnd 2:** 1dc/1sc in each of next 26dc/26sc. Rep last rnd until entire leg measures 11cm (4¼in), turn. Now work in rows.

**Leg shaping:**

**Next row:** 1ch, miss next dc/sc, 1dc/1sc in each dc/sc to end (marker), turn (25dc/25sc).

Rep last row 8 times more (17dc/17sc).

**Next row:** 1ch, 1dc/1sc in each dc/sc across.

Fasten off.

Make another leg in the same way.

**Join legs:**

With WS out, join two legs at back and front gusset by working 1dc/1sc in each row-end edge from waist at centre front, down along centre front up along centre back to centre back waist. Turn out to RS.

**Waistband:**

At waist edge, join in yarn A to a dc/sc at centre back waist edge, work 1ch, 1dc/1sc in each dc/sc around waist (34dc/34sc).

**Next rnd:** 1dc/1sc in each dc/sc around, sl st to first dc/sc of rnd.

Fasten off.

## TO FINISH

Weave in all ends.

Thread the ribbon through the waistband, through first dc/sc after centre front seam, then every 3rd dc/sc around the waistband.

# Basic shoes

## SIZE

8cm (3¼in) long

## MATERIALS

Small amount of 4ply (fingering weight) wool and acrylic blend in pale blue

3.50mm (E-4) hook

Two 5mm (³⁄₁₆in) buttons

Blue thread for attaching buttons

## TENSION (GAUGE)
9 sts and 10 rows to 5cm (2in) over dc/sc.

## SHOES (make 2)
**Foundation row:** Beg at toe, make 2ch.
**Rnd 1:** 6dc/6sc in 2nd ch from hook.
**Rnd 2:** 2dc/2sc in each of next 6dc/6sc (12dc/12sc).
**Rnd 3:** *1dc/1sc in each of next 2dc/2sc, 2dc/2sc in next dc/sc, rep from * around (16dc/16sc).
**Rnd 4:** 1dc/1sc in each of next 16dc/16sc.
Rep last rnd twice more.
### Shape top of shoe:
**Rnd 7:** [Miss next dc/sc, 1dc/1sc in next dc/sc] 4 times, 1dc/1sc in each of next 8dc/8sc, turn (12dc/12sc).
Now work in rows.
### Shape upper:
**Row 1:** 1ch, 1dc/1sc in each of next 6dc/6sc, turn.
**Row 2:** 1ch, 2dc/2sc in first dc/sc, 1dc/1sc in each of next 3dc/3sc, 2dc/2sc in next dc/sc, 1dc/1sc in last dc/sc, turn (8dc/8sc).
**Row 3:** 1ch, 2dc/2sc in first dc/sc, 1dc/1sc in each of next 5dc/5sc, 2dc/2sc in next dc/sc, 1dc/1sc in last dc/sc, turn (10dc/10sc).
**Row 4:** 1ch, 2dc/2sc in first dc/sc, 1dc/1sc in each of next 7dc/7sc, 2dc/2sc in next dc/sc, 1dc/1sc in last dc/sc, turn (12dc/12sc).
**Row 5:** 1ch, 1dc/1sc in each of next 12dc/12sc, turn.
Rep last row twice more.
**Next rnd:** 1dc/1sc in first dc/sc of this row to join back of heel. Starting at heel, work 21dc/21sc evenly around upper edge of shoe, sl st in first dc/sc of rnd. Fasten off.
Sew up heel seam. Weave in ends.

## SHOE STRAPS (make 2)
**Foundation row:** Make 10ch.
**Row 1:** 1dc/1sc in 2nd ch from hook, 1dc/1sc in each ch across (9dc/9sc).
Fasten off, leaving tail ends long enough to sew strap to the shoe.

## TO FINISH
Join one side of the strap to dc/sc at upper shaping. Sew the other side of the strap in place with a button.

# Basic skirt

## SIZE
7cm (2¾in) long x 20cm (7¾in) in diameter around waist

## MATERIALS

One 50g ball of aran-weight (worsted) cotton in denim blue (MC)
6.50mm (K-10½) hook
One 8mm (⁵⁄₁₆in) button
Three 5mm (³⁄₁₆in) buttons for decoration (optional)
Thread for attaching buttons

## TENSION (GAUGE)

7 sts and 6½ rows to 5cm (2in) over dc/sc.

## SKIRT

**Foundation row:** Beg at the waist edge, make 24ch, turn.
**Row 1:** 1dc/1sc in 2nd ch from hook, 1dc/1sc in each ch across, turn (23dc/23sc).
**Row 2:** 1ch, 1dc/1sc in each dc/sc across, do not twist yarn, join with sl st in 1ch to form a ring. Now work in rows.
**Rnd 1:** 1dc/1sc in each dc/sc around (23dc/23sc).
**Rnd 2:** 1dc/1sc in each of next 23dc/23sc. Rep last rnd 5 times more, ending sl st in next dc/sc.
Fasten off.

## TO FINISH

At each side of the skirt at waist, pinch in 2dc/2sc to wrong side and catch them with a couple of stitches to create a dart. Sew a button at the back that is just large enough for a stitch to fasten over it and be secure.
Sew the three smaller buttons evenly down the front (optional).

# Basic hat

## SIZE

11cm (4¼in) in diameter

## MATERIALS

One 50g ball of aran-weight (worsted) wool and acrylic blend in light green (MC)
Small amount of DK-weight (light worsted) angora yarn in pale pink for brim (A)
5.00mm (H-8) hook

## TENSION (GAUGE)

9 sts and 8 rnds to 5cm (2in) using yarn MC over dc/sc.

## HAT

The crown and the brim are worked as one.
**Foundation row:** Beg at top of crown, using yarn MC, make 2ch.
**Rnd 1:** 6dc/6sc in 2nd ch from hook.

**Rnd 2:** 2dc/2sc in each of next 6dc/6sc (12dc/sc).

**Rnd 3:** *1dc/1sc in next dc/sc, 2dc/2sc in next dc/sc, rep from * around (18dc/18sc).

**Rnd 4:** *1dc/1sc in each of next 2dc/2sc, 2dc/2sc in next dc/sc, rep from * around (24dc/24sc).

**Rnd 5:** *1dc/1sc in each of next 3dc/3sc, 2dc/2sc in next dc/sc, rep from * around (30dc/30sc).

**Rnd 6:** *1dc/1sc in each of next 4dc/4sc, 2dc/2sc in next dc/sc, rep from * around (36dc/36sc).

**Shape sides:**

**Rnd 7:** 1tr/1dc in each of next 36dc/36sc.

**Rnd 8:** 1tr/1dc in each of next 36tr/36dc. Fasten off yarn MC with sl st in next tr/dc. Weave in end.

**Brim:**

Join in yarn A with sl st in sl st of last rnd.

**Rnd 9:** *Miss next tr/dc, 1tr/1dc in each of next 3tr/3dc, rep from * around (27tr/27dc).

**Rnd 10:** [Miss next tr/dc, 1tr/1dc in each of next 3tr/3dc] 6 times, miss next tr/dc, 1tr/1dc in each of last 2tr/2dc (20tr/20dc).

Fasten off.

Pull up centre loose end to close the ring, weave in ends, leaving a short loop at centre of hat.

# Hula Hula Lula

**Aloha! With her grass skirt and flowery lei, this Hawaiian doll brings a touch of paradise to any child's room. Sporting a red headband, a yellow orchid behind her ear and bangles, Lula loves to accessorize in colour.**

## Doll

### SIZE
42cm (16½in) tall x 50cm (19¾in) wide (arms outstretched)

### MATERIALS
One 50g ball of DK-weight (light worsted) alpaca and merino blend in pale brown or other suitable skin colour for doll's body (MC)
One 50g ball of DK-weight (light worsted) cotton yarn in black for hair (A)
3.50mm (H-8) hook
Small pieces of felt for eyes
Black thread for sewing on eyes
Two 6mm (¼in) black glass beads or similar for eyes
Pink embroidery thread for mouth
Polyester toy stuffing or wadding
Yarn needle

### TENSION (GAUGE)
9 sts and 9 rows to 5cm (2in) using MC yarn over dc/sc.

### HEAD, BODY, ARMS, FEET & LEGS
Using yarn MC, make the same as for Basic Doll (page 20).

## Clothes and accessories

### MATERIALS
Small amount of DK-weight (light worsted) acrylic and nylon blend in lilac for tankini bottom (A)
Small amount of DK-weight (light worsted) acrylic and nylon blend in turquoise for grass skirt waistband (B)
Small amount of DK-weight (light worsted) wool and mohair blend in bright green for grass skirt (C)
Small amount of 4ply (fingering weight) cotton and merino blend in watermelon pink for tankini top and headband (D)
Small amount of 4ply (fingering weight) cotton and merino blend in white for

tankini top (E)
Small amount of DK-weight (light worsted) wool in red for sandals (F)
Small amounts of DK-weight (light worsted) yarn in bright colours of your choice for flowers and bangles
4.00mm (G-6) hook
Three 5mm (³⁄₁₆in) buttons for decoration (optional)
Thread for attaching button

## TENSION (GAUGE)

12 sts and 10 rows to 5cm (2in) using yarn A over dc/sc.

## TANKINI BOTTOM

Using yarn A, make as Tankini Bottom (page 24).

## TANKINI TOP

**Foundation row:** Using yarn D, make 40ch.
**Row 2:** 1tr/1dc in 4th ch from hook, 1tr/1dc in each ch across, join with sl st in top of 3ch at beg of row to form ring, taking care not to twist the row (38tr/38dc).
Fasten off.
**Rnd 1:** Join in yarn E with sl st in last tr/dc, 1dc/1sc in each tr/dc around.
**Rnd 2:** 1dc/1sc in each dc/sc around.

Rep last rnd once more.
Fasten off.

## GRASS SKIRT

**Foundation row:** Using yarn B, make 27ch.
**Row 1:** 1dc/1sc in 2nd ch from hook, 1dc/1sc in each ch across, turn (26dc/26sc).
**Row 2:** 2ch (counts as 1ch and 1dc/1sc), miss first dc/sc to make buttonhole – 1dc/1sc in each dc/sc to end.
Fasten off.
Sew on button at front.
To join 'grass', cut 28cm (11in) lengths of yarn C. Taking one length at a time, bend in half and, using a crochet hook, pull the loop through a dc/sc stitch along the foundation row of the skirt waistband. Pass the cut ends through the loops, then pull the cut ends firmly so that the knot lies close to the dc/sc stitch. Continue with this fringing technique along the band.

## LEI

**Foundation row:** Using any colour for flower, make 7ch, join with sl st to form ring.
**Rnd 1:** Working over the tail end, 14dc/14sc into ring, sl st in first dc/sc

of rnd.

**Rnd 2:** 4ch, (4dtr/4tr tog, inserting hook twice in next dc/sc and twice in foll dc/sc, 3ch, 1dc/1sc in next dc/sc, 3ch) 4 times, 4dtr/4tr tog inserting hook as before, 3ch, sl st in first ch of rnd.
Fasten off. Draw up the centre hole a little, leaving a tiny hole for threading. Weave in all ends.

Make as many flowers as you want for the lei and thread onto a single length of yarn. We used a single yellow flower to tuck behind Lula's ear.

## HEADBAND
**Foundation row:** Using yarn E, make 38ch.
**Row 1:** 1dc/1sc in 2nd ch from hook, 1dc/1sc in each ch across (37dc/37sc).

Fasten off.
Sew up the row-end edges to join into a band. Weave in the ends.

## SANDALS (make 2)
### Sole:
**Foundation row:** Using yarn F, make 13 ch.
**Row 1:** 1dc/1sc in 2nd ch from hook, 1dc/1sc in each ch across, turn (12dc/12sc).
**Row 2:** 1ch, 1dc/1sc in each dc/sc across, turn.
Rep last row 7 times more.
Fasten off.
Fold into 3 layers across foundation and finishing rows, sew up to hold in place.
### Upper strap:
**Foundation row:** Using yarn F, make 9ch.
**Row 1:** 1dc/1sc in 2nd ch from hook, 1dc/1sc in each ch across, turn (8dc/8sc).
**Row 2:** 1ch, 1dc/1sc in each dc/sc across.
Fasten off.
Sew to each side of the sole (a little more to the front than the back).

## BANGLES
Using yarn colours of your choice, make bangles to fit around Lula's wrists from lengths of chain.

# Sailor Bear

**Ships ahoy! This little fella's had more than his fair share of excitement on the high seas. With his smart hat and tie, he's an invaluable treasure.**

## Bear

### SIZE
31cm (12¼in) tall x 35cm (13¾in) wide (arms outstretched)

### MATERIALS
One 50g ball of aran-weight (worsted) wool and mohair blend in cream for bear's body (MC)
Small amount of DK-weight (light worsted) wool in dark grey for nose (A)
5.00mm (H-8) hook
Black embroidery thread for attaching beads and for mouth
Two 6mm (¼in) black glass beads or similar for eyes
Polyester toy stuffing or wadding
Yarn needle

### TENSION (GAUGE)
9 sts and 8 rnds to 5cm (2in) using yarn MC over dc/sc.

### NOTE
Before beginning the second round in each section, place a marker or short length of contrasting yarn across your crochet and up against the loop on the hook and above the working yarn. Work Rnd 2 then slip the marker out and place it at the beginning of the next round and so on. The marker will indicate where each subsequent round starts.

### HEAD, BODY, ARMS & LEGS
Make as for Basic Bear (page 14) then make up in the same way.

## Sailor's trousers

### SIZE
17cm (6¾in) long x 23cm (9in) in diameter around waist

### MATERIALS
One 50g ball of aran-weight (worsted)

cotton yarn in variegated denim blue
(MC)
One 50g ball of aran-weight (worsted)
cotton yarn in white (A)
5.00mm (H-8) hook

## TENSION (GAUGE)
8 sts and 9 rows to 5cm (2in) using MC
over dc/sc.

## TROUSERS
Make as for Basic Trousers (see page 30)
without following the colour sequence
used to create stripes. Use the following
colour sequence instead:
**Foundation row and Row 1:** Yarn MC.
**Row 2 onwards:** Yarn A.
Cont in yarn A until you reach the
waistband, then change to yarn MC.

# Sailor's top

## SIZE
11cm (4¼in) long x 15cm (6in) wide

## MATERIALS
One 50g ball of aran-weight (worsted)
cotton in variegated denim blue (MC)
One 50g ball of aran-weight (worsted)

cotton in white (A)
Small amount of DK-weight (light
worsted) cotton in dark grey for tie (B)
5.00mm (H-8) hook
Yarn needle

## TENSION (GAUGE)
8 sts and 9 rows to 5cm (2in) using MC
over dc/sc.

## FRONT
**Foundation row:** Using yarn A, beg at
front waist edge, make 18ch.
**Row 1 (RS):** 1tr/1dc in 4th ch from
hook, 1tr/1dc in each ch across, turn
(16tr/16dc).
**Row 2:** 3ch (counts as first tr/dc), miss
first tr/dc, 1tr/1dc in each tr/dc across,
turn.
**Row 3:** Join in yarn MC, 1ch, 1dc/1sc in
each tr/dc across, turn (16dc/16sc).
**Row 4:** 1ch, 1dc/1sc in each dc/sc
across.**
Rep last row 10 times more.
**Shape left front 'V':**
**Row 15:** 1ch, 1dc/1sc in each of next
8dc/8sc, turn (8dc/8sc).
**Row 16:** Sl st in first dc/sc, 1ch, 1dc/1sc in
each of next 7dc/7sc, turn (7dc/7sc).
**Row 17:** 1ch, 1dc/1sc in each of next
5dc/5sc, miss next dc/sc, 1dc/1sc in next

dc/sc, turn (6dc/6sc).

**Row 18:** Sl st in first dc/sc, 1ch, 1dc/1sc in each of next 5dc/5sc, turn (5dc/5sc).

**Row 19:** 1ch, 1dc/1sc in each of next 3dc/3sc, miss next dc/sc, 1dc/1sc in next dc/sc, turn (4dc/4sc).

**Row 20:** Sl st in first dc/sc, 1ch, 1dc/1sc in each of next 3dc/3sc (3dc/3sc).

**Row 21:** 1ch, 1dc/1sc in each of next 3dc/3sc.

Fasten off.

### Shape right front 'V':

**Row 15:** With RS facing, join in yarn MC to centre front, counting in 8dc/8sc from side edge, 1ch, 1dc/1sc in each of next 8dc/8sc, turn (8dc/8sc).

**Row 16:** 1ch, 1dc/1sc in each of next 6dc/6sc, miss next dc/sc, 1dc/1sc in next dc/sc, turn (7dc/7sc).

**Row 17:** Sl st in first dc/sc, 1ch, 1dc/1sc in each of next 6dc/6sc, turn (6dc/6sc).

**Row 18:** 1ch, 1dc/1sc in each of next 4dc/4sc, miss next dc/sc, 1dc/1sc in next dc/sc, turn (5dc/5sc).

**Row 19:** Sl st in first dc/sc, 1ch, 1dc/1sc in each of next 4dc/4sc, turn (4dc/4sc).

**Row 20:** 1ch, 1dc/1sc in each of next 2dc/2sc, miss next dc/sc, 1dc/1sc in next dc/sc, turn (3dc/3sc).

**Row 21:** 1ch, 1dc/1sc in each of next 3dc/3sc.

Fasten off.

### BACK

Work as for front up to **.

Rep last row 15 times more.

### Shape back neck:

**Next row (WS):** 1ch, 1dc/1sc in each of next 5dc/5sc, turn.

**Next row:** Sl st in first dc/sc, 1ch, miss next dc/sc, 1dc/1sc in cach of next 3dc/3sc (3dc/3sc).

Fasten off.

**Next row:** With WS facing, miss centre 6dc/6sc, join in yarn MC to next dc/sc, 1ch, 1dc/1sc in same dc/sc, 1dc/1sc in each of next 4dc/4sc, turn (5dc/5sc).

**Next row:** 1ch, 1dc/1sc in each of next 2dc/2sc, miss next dc/sc, 1dc/1sc in next dc/sc (3dc/3sc). Fasten off.

Using backstitch, sew up the shoulder seams and up from waist edge 6cm (2½in) at each side.

### SLEEVES (make 2)

With RS facing, join in yarn MC in shoulder seam at armhole edge, 1ch, work 23dc/23sc evenly around armhole.

Place marker, cont working in rnds until sleeve measures 2.5cm (1in), ending with sl st in first dc/sc of previous rnd.

Fasten off. Weave in ends.

## TO FINISH

Weave in all ends.

With RS facing, join in yarn A at lower point of front 'V', work in dc/sc evenly around neck edge, sl st to first dc/sc. Fasten off.

## BOW FOR SHIRT FRONT

**Foundation row:** Using yarn B, make 19ch.

**Row 1:** 1dc/1sc in 2nd ch from hook, 1dc/1sc in each ch across (18dc/18sc). Fasten off.

Weave in ends, twist a loop, sew to front of shirt.

# Sailor's shoes

## SIZE

7cm (2¾in) x 4cm (1½in)

## MATERIALS

Small amount of DK-weight (light worsted) wool and acrylic blend in dark grey
5.00mm (H-8) hook
Yarn needle

## TENSION (GAUGE)

8 sts and 9 rows to 5cm (2in) over dc/sc.

## SHOES (make 2)

**Foundation row:** Beg at toe, make 2ch.

**Rnd 1:** 6dc/6sc in 2nd ch from hook.

**Rnd 2:** 2dc/2sc in each of next 6dc/6sc (12dc/12sc).

**Rnd 3:** 2dc/2sc in each of next 12dc/12sc (24dc/24sc).

**Rnd 4:** 1dc/1sc in each of next 24dc/24sc. Rep last rnd 4 times more.

**Shape top of shoe:**

**Rnd 9:** 1ch, (miss next dc/sc, sl st in next dc/sc) 6 times, 1dc/1sc in each of next 12dc/12sc, turn (18 sts).

Now work in rows.

**Shape sides:**

**Next row:** 1ch, 1dc/1sc in each of next 12dc/12sc, turn.

Rep last row 4 times more.

Fasten off. Sew up the heel seam.

**Top of shoe:**

Join in yarn at heel seam, 2ch, work in htr/hdc evenly around top edge of shoe, sl st in top of 2ch.

Fasten off. Weave in ends.

# Sailor's cap

## SIZE

17cm (6¾in) in diameter

## MATERIALS

Small amount of DK-weight (light worsted) wool in white (A)

Small amount of DK-weight (light worsted) wool and acrylic blend in dark grey (B)

Small amount of DK-weight (light worsted) wool in bright red for hat tassel (C)

5.00mm (H-8) hook

Yarn needle

## TENSION (GAUGE)

8 sts and 9 rows to 5cm (2in) using MC yarn over dc/sc.

## CAP

**Foundation row:** Beg at top, using yarn A, make 2ch.

**Rnd 1:** 8dc/8sc in 2nd ch from hook.

**Rnd 2:** *1dc/1sc in next dc/sc, 2dc/2sc in next dc/sc, rep from * around (12dc/12sc).

**Rnd 3:** *1dc/1sc in each of next 2dc/2sc, 2dc/2sc in next dc/sc, rep from * around (16dc/16sc).

**Rnd 4:** *1dc/1sc in each of next 3dc/3sc, 2dc/2sc in next dc/sc, rep from * around (20dc/20sc).

**Rnd 5:** *1dc/1sc in each of next 4dc/4sc, 2dc/2sc in next dc/sc, rep from * around (24dc/24sc).

**Rnd 6:** *1dc/1sc in each of next 5dc/5sc, 2dc/2sc in next dc/sc, rep from * around (28dc/28sc).

**Rnd 7:** *1dc/1sc in each of next 6dc/6sc, 2dc/2sc in next dc/sc, rep from * around (32dc/32sc).

**Rnd 8:** 1dc/1sc in each of next 32dc/32sc. Rep last rnd twice more.

**Rnd 11:** *1dc/1sc in next dc/sc, miss next dc/sc, rep from * around (16dc/16sc). Fasten off.

**Rnd 12:** Join in yarn B with sl st in last dc/sc, 1ch, 1dc/1sc in each of next 16dc/16sc.

Rep last rnd once more.

Fasten off.

**Rnd 14:** Join in yarn MC with sl st in last dc/sc, 1ch, 1dc/1sc in each of next 16dc/16sc.

Fasten off. Weave in ends.

## TO FINISH

To make the tassel, cut short lengths of yarn C, bend in half, and hook the loop through any dc/sc at the top of the cap. Pass the raw ends through the loop, and pull through the loop to lie flat against the cap. Bunch up the strands, then tie them around the middle with another length of yarn C. Trim if necessary. Sew the cap to the bear's head.

# Molly the Mermaid

**Elegant and serene, Molly's flowing locks and beautiful blue eyes make her a sight to behold at sea or on land. Join her in her underwater palace and watch the hours float by.**

## Mermaid

### SIZE
41cm (16in) tall x 50cm (19¾in) wide (arms outstretched)

### MATERIALS
One 50g ball of DK-weight (light worsted) cotton in pale pink for mermaid's body (MC)
One 50g ball of DK-weight (light worsted) cotton and acrylic blend in light green for tail (A)
One 50g ball of DK-weight (light worsted) cotton and acrylic blend in lime green for tail fins (B)
Small amounts of DK-weight (light worsted) wool in two shades of green for tail ruffles in order of making (C)
Small amount of 4ply (fingering weight) cotton in pink for shell in hair and for mouth (D)
One 50g ball of DK-weight (light worsted) cotton in banana yellow for hair (E)

2.50mm (C-2) and 3.50mm (E-4) hooks
Small pieces of felt for eyes
Black and pink embroidery thread for sewing on eyes and mouth detail
Two 6mm (¼in) black glass beads or similar for eyes
Polyester toy stuffing or wadding
Yarn needle

### TENSION (GAUGE)
12 sts and 12 rnds to 5cm (2in) using 3.50mm (E-4) hook and MC yarn over dc/sc.

### NOTE
Before beginning the second round in each section, place a marker or short length of contrasting yarn across your crochet and up against the loop on the hook and above the working yarn. Work Rnd 2, then slip the marker out and place it at the beginning of the next round and so on. The marker will indicate where each subsequent round starts.

## HEAD, BODY & ARMS

Using yarn MC and 3.50mm (E-4) hook, make the same as for Basic Doll (page 20).

## NOTE:

For the mermaid, make only the trunk of the Basic Doll.

## TAIL

**Foundation rnd:** Using yarn A and 3.50mm (E-4) hook, beg at tip of tail, make 3ch, join with a sl st to form ring.

**Rnd 1:** Working over tail end, 1dc/1sc in next ch, 2dc/2sc in next ch, 1dc/1sc in last ch (4dc/4sc).

**Rnd 2:** 1dc/1sc in each of next 4dc/4sc.

**Rnd 3:** 2dc/2sc in each of next 4dc/4sc (8dc/8sc).

**Rnd 4:** 1dc/1sc in each of next 8dc/8sc. Rep last rnd once more.

**Rnd 6:** 1dc/1sc in next dc/sc, 2dc/2sc in next dc/sc, 1dc/1sc in each of next 3dc/3sc, 2dc/2sc in next dc/sc, 1dc/1sc in each of next 2dc/2sc (10dc/10sc).

**Rnd 7:** 1dc/1sc in each of next 10dc/10sc. Rep last rnd once more.

**Rnd 9:** [1dc/1sc in each of next 2dc/2sc, 2dc/2sc in next dc/sc] 3 times, 1dc/1sc in next dc/sc (13dc/13sc).

**Rnd 10:** 1dc/1sc in each of next 13dc/13sc.

Rep last rnd once more.

**Rnd 12:** [1dc/1sc in each of next 3dc/3sc, 2dc/2sc in next dc/sc] 3 times, 1dc/1sc in next dc/sc (16dc/16sc).

**Rnd 13:** 1dc/1sc in each of next 16dc/16sc.

Rep last rnd once more.

**Rnd 15:** [1dc/1sc in each of next 7dc/7sc, 2dc/2sc in next dc/sc] twice (18dc/18sc).

**Rnd 16:** 1dc/1sc in each of next 18dc/18sc.

Rep last rnd once more.

**Rnd 18:** [1dc/1sc in each of next 8dc/8sc, 2dc/2sc in next dc/sc] twice (20dc/20sc).

**Rnd 19:** 1dc/1sc in each of next 20dc/20sc.

Rep last rnd once more.

**Rnd 21:** 1ch, 1dc/1sc in each of next 20dc/20sc, turn (21 sts).

## Shell pattern:

**Row 1:** 4ch, 3dtr/3tr in first dc/sc, [miss 3dc/3sc, 1dc/1sc in next dc/sc, miss 3dc/3sc, 7dtr/7tr in next dc/sc] twice, miss 3dc/3sc, 1dc/1sc in 1ch at beg of previous row, turn.

**Row 2:** 4ch, 3dtr/3tr in first dc/sc, [miss 3dtr/3tr, 1dc/1sc in next dtr/tr (the centre dtr/tr of 7), miss 3dtr/3tr, 7dtr/7tr in next dc/sc] twice, miss 3dtr/3tr, 1dc/1sc in 4th of 4ch at beg of previous row, turn.

Rep last row 5 times more.
Fasten off.

## TAIL RUFFLE
**Make 4 ruffles:** one in yarn A, one in yarn B and two in yarn C.
**Foundation row:** Using appropriate yarn and using 3.50mm (E-4) hook, make 30ch.
**Row 1:** 1dc/1sc in 2nd ch from hook, 1dc/1sc in each ch across, turn (29dc/29sc).
**Row 2:** 1ch, 1dc/1sc in each dc/sc across (29dc/29sc).
**Row 3:** 1ch, 1dc/1sc in first dc/sc, *miss 1dc/1sc, 5tr/5dc in next dc/sc, miss 1dc/1sc, 1dc/1sc in next dc/sc, rep from * to end.
Fasten off.

## TAIL FINS (make 2)
**Foundation rnd:** Using yarn B and 3.50mm (E-4) hook, beg at tip of tail, make 4ch, join with a sl st to form ring.
**Rnd 1:** Working over tail end, [1dc/1sc in next ch, 2dc/2sc in next ch] twice (6dc/6sc).
**Rnd 2:** 1dc/1sc in each of next 6dc/6sc.
**Rnd 3:** [1dc/1sc in next dc/sc, 2dc/2sc in next dc/sc] 3 times (9dc/9sc).
**Rnd 4:** 1dc/1sc in each of next 9dc/9sc.

**Rnd 5:** [1dc/1sc in next dc/sc, 2dc/2sc in next dc/sc] 4 times, 1dc/1sc in next dc/sc (13dc/13sc).
**Rnd 6:** 1dc/1sc in each dc/sc around.
**Rnd 7:** [1dc/1sc in next dc/sc, 2dc/2sc in next dc/sc] 6 times, 1dc/1sc in next dc/sc (19dc/19sc).
**Rnd 8:** 1dc/1sc in each of next 19dc/19sc. Rep last rnd 5 times more.
**Rnd 14:** [1dc/1sc in each of next 2dc/2sc, miss next dc/sc] 6 times, 1dc/1sc in next dc/sc (13dc/13sc).
**Rnd 15:** 1dc/1sc in each of next 13dc/13sc.
**Rnd 16:** [1dc/1sc in next dc/sc, miss next dc/sc] 6 times, 1dc/1sc in next dc/sc (7dc/7sc).
**Rnd 17:** 1dc/1sc in each of next 7dc/7sc. Rep last rnd once more. Fasten off.

## SHELL (IN HAIR)
**Foundation row:** Using yarn D and 2.50mm (C-2) hook, make 6ch.
**Row 1:** 1dc/1sc in 2nd ch from hook, 1dc/1sc in each ch across (5dc/5sc).
**Row 2:** 1ch, 1dc/1sc in each dc/sc across (5dc/5sc).
**Row 3:** 1ch, 1dc/1sc in first dc/sc, miss 1dc/1sc, 5tr/5dc in next dc/sc, miss 1dc/1sc, 1dc/1sc in next dc/sc.
Fasten off.

## TO FINISH

Follow instructions for Basic Doll (page 20).

Sew the finishing row of the first tail ruffle to the top of the tail (the wavy edges should lie over the top of the tail). Sew up the tail along the back seam. Ease to fit the top of the tail to the bottom edge of the body and oversew in place. Sew on the other three ruffles so that they fall one-third of the way down the tail. At the tip of the tail, oversew the two tail fins at either side of the tail. To sew on hair, cut yarn E into lengths of 36cm (14¼in) and follow instructions for Basic Doll (page 24). Sew the hair shell in place at the side of the head.

## Tankini

## MATERIALS

Small amount of DK-weight (light worsted) wool and acrylic blend in pale blue (MC)
Small amount of DK-weight (light worsted) wool and acrylic blend in lilac for ruffle (A)
3.50mm (E-4) hook
Yarn needle

## BACK AND FRONT

**Foundation row:** Using yarn A, beg with the ruffle, make 50ch.
**Row 1:** 1dc/1sc in 2nd ch from hook, 1dc/1sc in next ch, *3ch, miss 1ch, 1dc/1sc in each of next 3ch, rep from * to last 3ch, 3ch, miss 1ch, 1dc/1sc in each of last 2ch, turn.
**Row 2:** 1ch, 1dc/1sc in first dc/sc, *miss 1dc/1sc, 5tr/5dc in next 3ch loop, miss 1dc/1sc, 1dc/1sc in next dc/sc, rep from * to end, turn.
**Row 3:** 5ch, miss first dc/sc and next tr/dc, *1dc/1sc in each of next 3tr/3dc, 3ch, miss (1tr/1dc, 1dc/1sc and 1tr/1sc), rep from * to last 5tr/5dc group, 1dc/1sc in each of next 3tr/3dc, 2ch, miss 1tr/1dc, 1tr/1dc in last dc/sc.
Fasten off.
With RS facing, join in yarn MC to corner of foundation row edge and work 34dc/34sc evenly across straight edge of ruffle, turn.
**Next row:** 1ch, 1dc/1sc in each of next 34dc/34sc, turn.
Rep last row once more.
Fasten off.

## STRAPS (make 2)

In yarn MC, make 12ch.
Fasten off.

## TO FINISH

Sew up the back seam, oversew the straps at the arm positions. Fit the top onto the mermaid for accurate positioning.

# Mirror

## MATERIALS

Small amount of 4ply (fingering weight) cotton in hot pink for back and handle (MC)
Small amount of 4ply (fingering weight) metallic yarn in silver for glass (A)
2.50mm (C-2) hook
Yarn needle

## MIRROR BACK

**Foundation row:** Using yarn MC, make 2ch.
**\*\*Rnd 1:** 6dc/6sc in 2nd ch from hook, join with sl st to first dc/sc to form ring (6dc/6sc).
**Rnd 2:** 1dc/1sc in each of next 6dc/6sc.
**Rnd 3:** [1dc/1sc in next dc/sc, 2dc/2sc in next dc/sc] 3 times (9dc/9sc).\*\*
**Rnd 4:** 2dc/2sc in each of next 9dc/9sc, sl st in first dc/sc of rnd (18dc/sc).

### Handle:

Make 10ch.
**Row 1:** 1tr/1dc in 4th ch from hook, 1tr/1dc in each of next 4ch, 1htr/1hdc in next ch, [1dc/1sc, 1ch, 1dc/1sc] in last ch. Fasten off.
Weave in ends to stabilize handle.

## MIRROR GLASS

**Foundation row:** Using yarn A, make 2ch.
Work as for Mirror Back from \*\* to \*\*.
Fasten off.
Sew the glass to the mirror back.
Sew the mirror handle to the mermaid's right hand.

# Nursery Toys

**A few nursery toys will add warmth to your child's bedroom and help send your tot to the land of sweet dreams.**

# Magical Finger Puppets

**Easy to make, these four magical characters get a thumb's up on fun! Create the ones here or design your own characters from your favourite film or book. They really are a handful!**

## SIZE
8 x 7cm (3 x 2¾in) tall

## MATERIALS

### WIZARD
Small amount of DK-weight (light worsted) angora and wool blend in navy blue for robe and hat (MC)
Small amount of 4ply (fingering weight) merino in pale pink for face (A)
Small amount of DK-weight (light worsted) wool in white for beard (B)
4.00mm (G-6) hook
Black sewing thread for eyes
Small amount of silver metallic yarn for decoration on robe and hat

### WITCH
Small amount of DK-weight (light worsted) cotton in black for robe and hat (MC)
Small amount of 4ply (fingering weight) merino in pale pink for face (A)
Small amount of 4ply (fingering weight) wool in grass green for hair (B)
4.00mm (G-6) hook
Black sewing thread for eyes and nose
Orange sewing thread for mouth

### OWL
Small amount of DK-weight (light worsted) wool and acrylic blend in cream for body (MC)
Small amount of DK-weight (light worsted) wool in cream for outer eyes (A)
4.00mm (G-6) hook
Small pieces of yellow felt
Two white feathers
Black sewing thread for eyes and nose

### WALRUS CALF
Small amount of 4ply (fingering weight) angora and wool blend in brown (MC)
Held together with small amount of 4ply (fingering weight) mohair and silk blend in cream (A)
Small amount of DK-weight (light worsted) yarn in cream for tusks

4.00mm (G-6) hook
Embroidery thread for sewing eyes, nose and mouth
Two 6mm (¼in) black glass beads or similar for eyes

## TENSION (GAUGE)
12 sts and 12 rows to 5cm (2in) using 4.00mm hook and yarn MC over dc/sc. (NB: hold yarns MC and A together for Walrus Calf.)

## NOTE
Before beginning the second round in each section, place a marker or short length of contrasting yarn across your crochet and up against the loop on the hook and above the working yarn. Work Rnd 2, then slip the marker out and place it at the beginning of the next round and so on. The marker will indicate where each subsequent round starts.

# Wizard, witch and owl

## HEAD & BODY
**Foundation row:** Using yarn MC, make 12ch. Taking care not to twist the chain, join into a ring with sl st in first ch of rnd.
**Rnd 1:** 1ch, 1dc/1sc in each ch around (12dc/12sc).
**Rnd 2:** 1dc/1sc in each dc/sc around. Rep last row until the body measures 5cm (2in).
**Shape neck:**
**Next rnd:** *Miss next dc/sc, 1dc/1sc in each of next 2dc/2sc, rep from * around (8dc/8sc).
**Next rnd:** 1dc/1sc in each dc/sc around. Rep last rnd once more.
**Wizard and witch only:**
Fasten off yarn MC with sl st in next dc/sc, join in yarn A with sl st in same place, make 1ch.
**Wizard, witch and owl:**
**Next rnd:** 1dc/1sc in each dc/sc around (8dc/8sc).
**Next rnd:** *2dc/2sc in next dc/sc, 1dc/1sc in each of next 3dc/3sc, rep from * once more (10dc/10sc).
**Next rnd:** *2dc/2sc in next dc/sc, 1dc/1sc in each of next 4dc/4sc, rep from * once more (12dc/12sc).
**Next rnd:** *2dc/2sc in next dc/sc, 1dc/1sc in each of next 5dc/5sc, rep from * once more (14dc/14sc).
**Wizard and witch only:**
Use this to coil around in a flat twist at the end of the head. Sew in place to secure.
Proceed to instructions for hat.

**Owl only:**
*Miss next dc/sc, 1dc/1sc in each of next 6dc/6sc, rep from * once more (12dc/12sc).

**Next rnd:** *Miss next dc/sc, 1dc/1sc in each of next 2dc/2sc, rep from * around (8dc/8sc).

**Next rnd:** *Miss next dc/sc, 1dc/1sc in next dc/sc, rep from * around until the ring is closed.
Fasten off. Weave in ends.

## HAT – WIZARD & WITCH ONLY

Fasten off yarn A with sl st in next dc/sc, join in yarn MC with sl st in same place, 1ch.

**Next rnd:** 1dc/1sc in each dc/sc around.
**Next rnd:** *Miss next dc/sc, 1dc/1sc in next dc/sc, rep from * around (7dc/7sc).
**Next rnd:** 1dc/1sc in each dc/sc around.
Rep last rnd twice more.
**Next rnd:** *Miss next dc/sc, 1dc/1sc in next dc/sc, rep from * around until the ring is closed.
Fasten off. Weave in ends.

**Witch's hat brim:**
**Foundation row:** Using yarn MC, make 15 ch.
**Row 1:** 1dc/1sc in 2nd ch from hook, 2dc/2sc in next ch, *1dc/1sc in next ch, 2dc/2sc in next ch; rep from * to end.

Fasten off. Sew the brim to the top of the head – where the hat rim colour begins.

## WIZARD & WITCH'S CLOAKS

**Foundation row:** Beg at the top of collar, using yarn MC, make 11ch.
**Row 1:** 1dc/1sc in 2nd ch from hook, 1dc/1sc in each of next 7ch, miss last ch, turn (8dc/8sc).
**Row 2:** Sl st in first dc/sc, 1ch, 1dc/1sc in each of next 6dc/6sc, miss last dc/sc, turn (6dc/6sc).
**Row 3:** 1ch, 1dc/1sc in each dc/sc across, turn.
Rep last row 3 times more.
**Row 7:** 2ch, 1dc/1sc in 2nd ch from hook, 1dc/1sc in each dc/sc to last dc/sc, 2dc/2sc in last dc/sc, turn (8dc/8sc).
Rep last row twice more (12dc/12sc).
Fasten off.
Work a border along each side edge starting at the hem corner and working up to the collar edge – 1dc/1sc in each dc/sc along.
Fasten off. Weave in ends.
Sew in place around the neck edge of the body, leaving the upper collar edge free around the back of the head.
Using 2 short lengths of MC, make a tie at each side of the collar and tie at the front of the cloak.

Using silver metallic yarn, sew a few stars by working 3 straight stitches across each other onto the Wizard's robes, cloak and hat.

## TO FINISH
### WIZARD & WITCH
Using double-thickness black sewing thread, sew two eyes on the front of the face.

Work a split-stitch mouth on the Witch's face using a length of orange sewing thread.

In cream yarn, work 2 straight stitches on the Wizard's face for eyebrows.

For the Wizard's beard, cut 3cm (1½in) lengths of yarn B. Thread half of one length through a stitch on the face at the beard position. Reinsert, then re-emerge the needle into the same crochet stitch – the thread should be secure. Trim if necessary. Work a few more lengths in the same way, depending on how bushy you want the beard to be.

For the Witch's hair, cut 3cm (1½in) lengths of yarn B and attach to the back of the head, under the hat brim, in the same way.

### OWL
Using outer eye yarn A, make 6ch, join into a ring with a sl st in first ch. Fasten off. Make another the same and sew both in place onto the front of the head. Using black thread, sew two eyes into the centre of these outer eyes – making the eyes bigger than those of the wizard's and witch's. Cut out a 6mm (¼in) equilateral triangle of felt for the beak. Sew this onto the owl's face with two black stitches for the nostrils. Poke the ends of the feathers into the owl's neck at the side of the body. Sew in place.

# Walrus calf

## HEAD & BODY

**Foundation row:** Beg at the head, using yarns MC and A together, make 2ch.

**Rnd 1:** 6dc/6sc in 2nd ch from hook.

**Rnd 2:** [1dc/1sc in next dc/sc, 2dc/2sc in next dc/sc] 3 times (9dc/9sc).

**Rnd 3:** 1dc/1sc in each dc/sc around. Rep last rnd 3 times more.

**Rnd 7:** [1dc/1sc in next dc/sc, 2dc/2sc in next dc/sc] 4 times, 1dc/1sc in last dc/sc (13dc/13sc).

**Rnd 8:** 1dc/1sc in each dc/sc around. Rep last rnd 3 times more.

**Rnd 12:** [1dc/1sc in each of next 3dc/3sc, 2dc/2sc in next dc/sc] 3 times, 1dc/1sc in last dc/sc (16dc/16sc).

**Rnd 13:** 1dc/1sc in each dc/sc around. Rep last rnd once more.

**Rnd 15:** *1dc/1sc in next dc/sc, miss next dc/sc, rep from * around (8dc/8sc). Rep last rnd twice more (2dc/2sc). Fasten off. Weave in ends.

## CHEEKS (make 2)

Using yarn MC, make 7ch. Fasten off. Use this to coil around in a flat twist at the end of head. Sew in place to secure.

## FLIPPERS (make 2)

**Foundation row:** In yarn MC, beg at the part of the fin that is later sewn to the body, make 5ch.

**Row 1:** 1dc/1sc in 2nd ch from hook, 1dc/1sc in each of next 3ch, turn (4dc/4sc).

**Row 2:** 1ch, 1dc/1sc in each dc/sc across, turn.

**Row 3:** 1ch, 1dc/1sc in each of next 3dc/3sc, turn (3dc/3sc).

**Row 4:** 1ch, 1dc/1sc in each dc/sc across, turn.

**Row 5:** 1ch, 1dc/1sc in each of next 2dc/2sc, turn (2dc/2sc).

**Row 6:** 1ch, miss next dc/sc, 1dc/1sc in last dc/sc. Fasten off.

## TO FINISH

Sew on the two beads for the eyes behind the cheeks. Cut two short lengths of cream yarn and sew them securely in place under the cheeks for tusks. Sew on the flippers with the pointed end facing away from the head. Weave in ends.

# Chunky Building Blocks

It's a block party! Learning your A-B-Cs from your 1-2-3s is made super-easy with these pastel blocks. This project is a great way to use up any leftover yarn from other projects.

## SIZE
All blocks are different sizes.

## MATERIALS
Small amounts of leftover yarns in bright and pastel colours for blocks
Small amounts of any DK-weight yarn for letters and numbers
5.00mm (H-8) hook for letters and numbers; suitable hook sizes for yarn of your choice for blocks
Polyester toy stuffing or wadding
Yarn needle

## TENSION (GAUGE)
Tension is not important for this project.

## BLOCK
**Foundation row:** Using any yarn and a suitably sized hook, make 6ch.
**Row 1:** 1dc/1sc in 2nd ch from hook, 1dc/1sc in each ch across, turn (5dc/5sc).
**Rows 2–4:** 1ch, 1dc/1sc in each dc/sc across, turn (5dc/5sc).
**Rnd 5:** 1ch, 1dc/1sc in each of next 4dc/4sc, 3dc/3sc in next (corner) dc/sc, cont around edge making 3dc/3sc along left side, 3dc/3sc in corner, 3dc/3sc across bottom, 3dc/3sc in corner, 3dc/3sc along right side, 2dc/2sc in top right-hand corner, sl st to first dc/sc of rnd.
Weave in ends. Make 5 more squares.

## LETTERS & NUMBERS
Decide on a letter or number. Make enough chain to twist and curve into that shape, then stitch the chain down onto one or more of the cube faces to secure the shape. For example: For number '3', using 5.00mm (H-8) hook, make 18ch, fasten off, leaving a long tail end to sew onto a cube face.

## TO FINISH
Sew squares together along outside edges, WS together, and stuff before closing the cube along last edge.

# Plush Car and Van

**Make a chunky, bright blue bubble car and butter-yellow van, or try crocheting one in racy red, marmalade orange or bubblegum pink. Pick a colour to suit your mood — or your child's room!**

## Car

### SIZE
20cm (7¾in) long x 11cm (4¼in) wide

### MATERIALS
One 50g ball of aran-weight (worsted) wool in bright blue for car (MC)
Small amount of aran-weight (worsted) wool in cream for roof (A)
One 50g ball of aran-weight (worsted) chenille yarn in black for tyres (B)
Small amount of aran-weight (worsted) cotton in yellow for headlights (C)
Small amount of dark grey yarn for window and door detail
Small amount of light grey yarn for door handle detail
4.00mm (G-6) and 5.00mm (H-8) hooks
Polyester toy stuffing or wadding
Yarn needle

### TENSION (GAUGE)
9 sts and 10 rnds to 5cm (2in) using 5.00mm (H-8) hook and MC yarn over dc/sc.

### NOTE
Before beginning the second round in each section, place a marker or short length of contrasting yarn across your crochet and up against the loop on the hook and above the working yarn. Work Rnd 2, then slip the marker out and place it at the beginning of the next round and so on. The marker will indicate where each subsequent round starts.

### SIDES (make 2)
**Foundation row:** Beg at the back of the car, using yarn MC and 5.00mm (H-8) hook, make 8ch.
**Row 1:** 1dc/1sc in 2nd ch from hook, 1dc/1sc in each ch across, turn (7dc/7sc).
**Row 2:** 1ch, 1dc/1sc in each dc/sc to last dc/sc, 2dc/2sc in last dc/sc, turn

(8dc/8sc).

**Row 3:** 2ch, 1dc/1sc in 2nd ch from hook, 1dc/1sc in each dc/sc across (9dc/9sc). Rep last 2 rows once more (11dc/11sc).

**Row 6:** 1ch, 1dc/1sc in each of next 11dc/11sc across, turn.

**Row 7:** 2ch, 1dc/1sc in 2nd ch from hook, 1dc/1sc in each dc/sc across (12dc/12sc).

**Row 8:** 1ch, 1dc/1sc in each of next 12dc/12sc across, turn.

Rep last row 8 times more.

**Row 17:** Sl st in first dc/sc, 1ch, 1dc/1sc in each dc/sc to end, turn (11dc/11sc).

**Row 18:** 1ch, 1dc/1sc in each dc/sc to last dc/sc, miss last dc/sc, turn (10dc/10sc).

Rep last 2 rows twice more (6dc/6sc).

**Row 23:** 1ch, 1dc/1sc in each of next 6dc/6sc, turn.

**Row 24:** 1ch, 1dc/1sc in each dc/sc to last dc/sc, miss last dc/sc, turn (5dc/5sc).

**Row 25:** 1ch, 1dc/1sc in each of next 5dc/5sc, turn.

Rep last row twice more.

Fasten off.

## BASE

**Foundation row:** With yarn MC and 5.00mm (H-8) hook, make 9ch.

**Row 1:** 1dc/1sc in 2nd ch from hook, 1dc/1sc in each ch across, turn (8dc/8sc).

**Row 2:** 1ch, 1dc/1sc in each dc/sc across,

turn. Rep last row 17 times more, or until the length of the base matches the length of one of the sides.

## ROOF

**Foundation row:** With yarn MC and 5.00mm (H-8) hook, make 9ch.

**Row 1:** 1dc/1sc in 2nd ch from hook, 1dc/1sc in each ch across, turn (8dc/8sc).

**Row 2:** 1ch, 1dc/1sc in each dc/sc across, turn.

Rep last row 7 times more, fasten off yarn MC with sl st.

Join in yarn A with sl st in sl st of previous row.

**Row 10:** 1ch, 1dc/1sc in each dc/sc across, turn.

Rep last row 9 times more, fasten off yarn A with sl st.

Join in yarn MC with sl st in sl st of previous row.

Rep last row 7 times more, or until the length of the roof fits up the back, over the top, and down to the front along one of the car sides.

## TYRES (make 5)

**Foundation row:** Using yarn B and 5.00mm (H-8) hook, make 4ch.

**Rnd 1:** 8dc/8sc in 4th ch from hook, working over loose end – pull up tight

when the tyre is complete to close the ring.
**Rnd 2:** 2dc/2sc in each dc/sc around
(16dc/16sc).
**Rnd 3:** 1dc/1sc in each dc/sc around.
Rep last rnd twice more.
**Rnd 6:** [1dc/1sc in each of next 2dc/2sc,
miss next dc/sc] 5 times, 1dc/1sc in last
dc/sc (11dc/11sc).
**Rnd 7:** [1dc/1sc in next dc/sc, miss next
dc/sc] 5 times, 1dc/1sc in last dc/sc
(6dc/6sc).
Carefully turn out to RS.
**Rnd 8:** *Miss next dc/sc, 1dc/1sc in next
dc/sc, rep from * to end.
Fasten off.

## HEADLIGHTS (make 2)
**Foundation row:** Using yarn C and
5.00mm (H-8) hook, make 2ch.
**Rnd 1:** 6dc/6sc in 2nd ch from hook.
**Rnd 2:** 2dc/2sc in each dc/sc around
(12dc/12sc).
**Rnd 3:** 1dc/1sc in each dc/sc around
(12dc/12sc).
Rep last rnd once more.
**Rnd 5:** *Miss next dc/sc, 1dc/1sc in next
dc/sc, rep from * to end (6dc/6sc).
Carefully turn out to RS.
Rep last rnd once more.
Fasten off.

## TO FINISH
With RS facing, join each side to the
car 'roof'. Sew the two headlights onto
front of car. Using yarn A, sew 2 straight
stitches to each headlight for highlight.

With RS facing, sew the base to the rem
outer edges of the front, back and sides,
leaving a small gap for turning through.
Turn RS out, stuff, and close the gap.

Sew on the wheels – two each side and
one on the trunk, making sure the
wheels on opposite sides are equidistant.

Thread a yarn needle with a length of dark grey yarn. Work backstitch down sides for door and windows and across front for windscreen details, as seen in the photograph. Using light grey yarn, sew a straight stitch to each 'door' for handle detail.

# Van

## SIZE
24cm (9½in) long x 12cm (4¾in) wide

## MATERIALS
One 50g ball of chunky (bulky) acrylic yarn in bright yellow for van (MC)
One 50g ball of chunky (bulky) wool yarn in white for van roof (A)
One 50g ball of chunky (bulky) wool yarn in grey for wheels (B)
Small amount of chunky (bulky) wool and acrylic blend in grey for headlights and bumpers (C)
Small amount of DK-weight (light worsted) yarn in grey for window and door detail
4.00mm (G-6) and 6.50mm (K-10½) hooks
Polyester toy stuffing or wadding
Yarn needle

## TENSION (GAUGE)
7 sts and 6 rows to 5cm (2in) using 6.50mm (K-10½) hook and yarn MC over dc/sc.

## BACK
**Foundation row:** Using yarn MC and 6.50mm (K-10½) hook, make 11ch.
**Row 1:** 1dc/1sc in 2nd ch from hook, 1dc/1sc in each ch across, turn (10dc/10sc).
**Row 2:** 1ch, 1dc/1sc in each dc/sc to end, turn.
Rep last row 5 times more.
Change to yarn A, work 4 more rows as last row.
Fasten off.

## LEFT SIDE, TOP & RIGHT SIDE
**Foundation row:** Beg at left back, using yarn MC and 6.50mm (K-10) hook, make 19ch.
**Row 1:** Sl st in first ch, 1ch, 1dc/1sc in each ch across, turn (18dc/18sc).
**Row 2:** 1ch, 1dc/1sc in each dc/sc across, turn.
**Row 3:** Sl st in first dc/sc, 1ch, 1dc/1sc in each dc/sc across, turn (17dc/17sc).
**Row 4:** 1ch, 1dc/1sc in each dc/sc across, turn.
Rep last row 3 times more.

**Row 8:** Change to yarn A, sl st in first dc/sc, 1ch, 1dc/1sc in each dc/sc across (16dc/16sc).

Work 15 more rows as Row 4.

**Row 24:** Change to yarn MC, 1ch, 1dc/1sc in each dc/sc to last dc/sc, 2dc/2sc in last dc/sc (17dc/17sc).

Work 2 more rows as Row 4.

**Row 27:** 2ch, 1dc/1sc in 2nd ch from hook, 1dc/1sc in each dc/sc across, turn (18dc/18sc).

**Row 28:** 1ch, 1dc/1sc in each dc across, turn.

Rep last 2 rows once more (19dc/19sc).

Fasten off.

## FRONT

**Foundation row:** Using yarn MC and 6.50mm (K-10½) hook, make 13ch.

**Row 1:** 1dc/1sc in 2nd ch from hook, 1dc/1sc in each ch across (12dc/12sc).

**Row 2:** 1ch, 1dc/1sc in each dc/sc to end, turn.

Rep last row 7 times more.

**Row 10:** Sl st in first dc/sc, 1ch, 1dc/1sc in each of next 9dc/9sc, miss next dc/sc, 1dc/1sc in last dc/sc (10dc/10sc).

**Row 11:** Change to yarn A, 1ch, 1dc/1sc in each dc/sc across.

Fasten off.

## BASE

**Foundation row:** Using yarn MC and 6.50mm (K-10½) hook, make 11ch.

**Row 1:** 1dc/1sc in 2nd ch from hook, 1dc/1sc in each next ch across, turn (10dc/10sc).

**Row 2:** 1ch, 1dc/1sc in each dc/sc across, turn.

Rep last row 15 times more.

Fasten off.

**Shape front dart:**

**Foundation row:** Using yarn A and 6.50mm (K-10½) hook, make 12ch.

**Row 1:** 1dc/1sc in 2nd ch from hook, 1dc/1sc in each ch across, turn (11dc/11sc).

**Row 2:** 1ch, 1dc/1sc in each dc/sc across, turn.

Rep last row twice more.

**Row 5:** Sl st in first dc/sc, 1ch, 1dc/1sc in each of next 8dc/8sc, miss next dc/sc, 1dc/1sc in last dc/sc, turn (9dc/9sc).

**Row 6:** Sl st in first dc/sc, 1ch, 1dc/1sc in each of next 6dc/6sc, miss next dc/sc, 1dc/1sc in last dc/sc, turn (7dc/7sc).

**Row 7:** Sl st in first dc/sc, 1ch, 1dc/1sc in each of next 4dc/4sc, miss next dc/sc, 1dc/1sc in last dc/sc, turn (5dc/5sc).

**Row 8:** Sl st in first dc/sc, 1ch, 1dc/1sc in each of next 2dc/2sc, miss next dc/sc, 1dc/1sc in last dc/sc, turn (3dc/3sc).

**Row 9:** Sl st in first dc/sc, miss next dc/
sc, 1dc/1sc in last dc/sc (1dc/1sc).
Fasten off.
Join yarn MC to 1ch at corner of
V-shaped dart, work 1dc/1sc in row ends
down two long sides to point of V.
Fasten off, leaving a long tail end for
sewing the dart to the front of the van.

## WHEELS (make 5)

**Foundation row:** Using yarn B and
6.50mm (K-10½) hook, make 4ch.
**Rnd 1:** 10dc/10sc in 4th ch from hook.
**Rnd 2:** 2dc/2sc in each dc/sc around
(20dc/20sc).
**Rnd 3:** 1dc/1sc in each dc/sc around.
Rep last rnd once more.
**Rnd 5:** [Miss next dc/sc, 1dc/1sc in each

of next 2dc/2sc] 6 times, miss next dc/sc, 1dc/1sc in last dc/sc (13dc/13sc).
**Rnd 6:** [Miss next dc/sc, 1dc/1sc in next dc/sc] 6 times, miss last dc/sc (6dc/6sc). Fasten off.

## HEADLIGHTS (make 2)
**Foundation row:** Using yarn C and 4.00mm (G-6) hook, make 4ch.
**Rnd 1:** 8tr/8dc in 4th ch from hook, sl st in top of first tr/dc to form ring. Fasten off, leaving long tail end for sewing to car.

## BUMPERS (make 2)
**Foundation row:** Using yarn C and 4.00mm (G-6) hook, make 21ch.
**Row 1:** 1dc/1sc in 2nd ch from hook, 1dc/1sc in each ch across, turn (20dc/20sc).
**Row 2:** 1ch, 1dc/1sc in each dc/sc across, turn.
Rep last row 3 times more.

Fasten off. Roll up across the length as you would a sleeping bag, then sew along one long end to secure.

## TO FINISH
Using a blunt-ended yarn needle and MC yarn, backstitch throughout. Sew the dart to the front of the van. Sew on the two headlights. With RS facing, join the front to the van sides, join the back, then the base, leaving a small gap at the front for turning through. Stuff the van, then sew up the gap. Sew on the back and front bumpers and then the wheels, adding the fifth wheel to the bumper.

Thread a yarn needle with a length of grey yarn. Work backstitch down sides for door and windows and across front for windscreen details. Using yarn A, embroider a French knot to each headlight for highlights. Using yarn C, embroider a door handle on each side.

# Planets and Rocket Mobile

**A charged yarn rocket gently navigates colourful planets to take your little one to the outer limits of dreamland. This is also the perfect project for using up your yarn stash!**

## SIZES
**Planets:** about 16cm (6½in) in diameter
**Rocket:** about 12cm (4¾in) long x 16cm (6½in) in diameter

## MATERIALS
Small amounts of chunky (bulky) yarn in hot pink, cream, pistachio green, shell pink, red, yellow, navy and sky blue for planets

Small amount of DK-weight (light worsted) yarn in raspberry for rocket (MC)

Small amount of DK-weight (light worsted) yarn in lemon for rocket (A)

Small amount of DK-weight (light worsted) yarn in brown for rocket base (B)

Small amount of DK-weight (light worsted) yarn in orange for flames

Small amount of DK-weight (light worsted) yarn in pale blue for hanging threads

4.00mm (G-6), 5.00mm (H-8) and 6.50mm (K-10½) hooks

Wooden hoop 20cm (8in) in diameter (or use one half of an embroidery hoop)

10m (11yd) length of 10mm (⅜in) blue velvet ribbon

Solvent-free glue stick for sticking the ribbon to the hoop

Three 10mm (⅜in) diameter buttons

Polyester toy stuffing or wadding

Yarn needle

## TENSION (GAUGE)
Tension is not important for this project.

## NOTE
Before beginning the second round in each section, place a marker or short length of contrasting yarn across your crochet and up against the loop on the hook and above the working yarn. Work Rnd 2, then slip the marker out and place it at the beginning of the next round and so on. The marker will indicate where each subsequent round starts.

## PLANETS (make 8: one in each planet yarn)

**Foundation row:** Using any chosen planet yarn and 6.50mm (K-10½) hook, make 4ch.

**Rnd 1:** 8dc/8sc in fourth ch from hook.

**Rnd 2:** 2dc/2sc in each dc/sc around (16dc/16sc).

**Rnd 3:** 1dc/1sc in each dc/sc around.

Rep last rnd twice more.

**Rnd 6:** [1dc/1sc in each next of 2dc/2sc, miss next dc/sc] 5 times, 1dc/1sc in last dc/sc (11dc/11sc).

**Rnd 7:** [1dc/1sc in next dc/sc, miss next dc/sc] 5 times, 1dc/1sc in last dc/sc (6dc/6sc).

Carefully turn out to RS and stuff the planet.

**Rnd 8:** *Miss next dc/sc, 1dc/1sc in next dc/sc, rep from * until ring is closed. Fasten off.

## ROCKET

**Foundation row:** Using yarn MC and 5.00mm (H-8) hook, make 2ch.

**Rnd 1:** 4dc/4sc in second ch from hook.

**Rnd 2:** 1dc/1sc in each of next 4dc/4sc.

**Rnd 3:** [1dc/1sc in next dc/sc, 2dc/2sc in next dc/sc] twice (6dc/6sc).

**Rnd 4:** [1dc/1sc in next dc/sc, 2dc/2sc in next dc/sc] 3 times (9dc/9sc).

**Rnd 5:** [1dc/1sc in next dc/sc, 2dc/2sc in next dc/sc] 4 times, 1dc/1sc in next dc/sc (13dc/13sc).

**Rnd 6:** [1dc/1sc in next dc/sc, 2dc/2sc in next dc/sc] 5 times, 1dc/1sc in next dc/sc (19dc/19sc).

**Rnd 7:** 1dc/1sc in each dc/sc around.

Rep last rnd twice more. Fasten off yarn MC with sl st in last dc/sc.

**Rnd 10:** Join in yarn A with sl st in same place as last sl st. Using 4.00mm (G-6) hook, 1dc/1sc in each dc/sc around.
Rep last rnd 5 times more.
Fasten off yarn A with sl st in last dc/sc.
**Rnd 16:** Join in yarn B with sl st in same place as last sl st. Using 5.00mm (H-8) hook, 1dc/1sc in each dc/sc around.
Rep last rnd 3 times more.
Fasten off.

## ROCKET BASE

**Foundation row:** Using yarn B and 5.00mm (H-8) hook, make 2ch.
**Rnd 1:** 4dc/4sc in second ch from hook.
**Rnd 2:** 2dc/2sc in each dc/sc around (8dc/8sc).
Rep last rnd twice more (32dc/32sc).
**Rnd 5:** 1dc/1sc in each dc/sc around.
Fasten off.

## TO FINISH THE ROCKET

Stuff the rocket. Ease the base of the rocket to just inside the bottom of the rocket base – about 6mm (¼in) in. With MC yarn and yarn needle, sew in place. Sew the buttons in a line down the front.

# Rocket boosters

Using yarn MC and 5.00mm (H-8) hook, make 25ch, then fasten off. Make another chain in the same manner. Wind one chain around your finger and sew to secure the coil. Do the same to the other chain. Sew each coil to the base of the rocket. Cut lengths of orange yarn and sew them to the inside of each booster for flames. Trim.

## TO FINISH THE MOBILE

Stick one end of the ribbon to the hoop to secure. Wrap the ribbon around the hoop until it is covered, then cut and secure the end with glue. Cut the remaining ribbon into five equal lengths for hanging strips. Glue one end of each of the five ribbon strips to the outside of the hoop at five evenly spaced points around the hoop. Knot the five lengths together at the other end.

Sew differing lengths of pale blue yarn to the top (finishing row) of each planet and to the rocket. Arranging the planets around the hoop as desired, knot each length of yarn securely to the hoop. Tie the rocket to the ribbon so that it hangs down from the centre of the mobile.

# Animal Kingdom

These projects come to life with a little imagination and make excellent presents for boys and girls of all ages. Join Larry the Lobster in his hunt for some freshwater fun, or drift off to sleep with Sir Waldorf Walrus on his afternoon nap. Or maybe joining Jenna the Giraffe at her afternoon tea party is more your scene?

# Jenna the Giraffe

With her snazzy, striped dress and fanciful scarf, Jenna is a gentle giant with a sweet tooth. This fun and whimsical giraffe boasts plenty of attitude and bold style. Subtle details – including her flirty embroidered eyelashes, spots along her neck, and a gingham bow around her horn – lend bundles of personality and character.

## Giraffe

### SIZE
49cm (19¼in) tall x 55cm (21¾in) wide with forelegs outstretched

### MATERIALS
One 50g ball of DK-weight (light worsted) angora and viscose blend yarn in orange (MC)
One 50g ball of DK-weight (light worsted) angora and viscose blend yarn in brown (A)
Small amount of DK-weight (light worsted) alpaca in brown for hooves and mane (B)
4.00mm (G-6) and 5.00mm (H-8) hooks
Pink and brown embroidery thread or fine yarn for mouth and nose
Two 6mm (¼in) black glass beads or similar for eyes
Black thread for eyelashes
30cm (12in) length of 6mm (¼in) ribbon

Polyester toy stuffing or wadding
Yarn needle

### TENSION (GAUGE)
9 sts and 8 rnds to 5cm (2in) using 5.00mm (H-8) hook and yarn MC over dc/sc.

### NOTE
Before beginning the second round in each section, place a marker or short length of contrasting yarn across your crochet and up against the loop on the hook and above the working yarn. Work Rnd 2, then slip the marker out and place it at the beginning of the next round and so on. The marker will indicate where each subsequent round starts.

### HEAD AND BODY
**Foundation row:** Beg at nose using yarn MC and 5.00mm (H-8) hook make 2ch.

**Rnd 1:** 6dc/6sc in 2nd ch from hook.

**Rnd 2:** [1dc/1sc in next dc/sc, 2dc/2sc in next dc/sc] 3 times (9dc/9sc).

**Rnd 3:** 1dc/1sc in each of next 9dc/9sc.

Rep last rnd twice more.

**Shape head:**

**Rnd 6:** [1dc/1sc in each of next 2dc/2sc, 2dc/2sc in next dc/sc] 3 times (12dc/12sc).

**Rnd 7:** 2dc/2sc in each of next 12dc/12sc (24dc/24sc).

**Rnd 8:** 1dc/1sc in each of next 24dc/24sc.

Rep last rnd twice more.

**Shape back of head:**

**Rnd 11:** *1dc/1sc in each of next 2dc/2sc, miss next dc/sc, rep from * around (16dc/16sc).

**Rnd 12:** *1dc/1sc in next dc/sc, miss next dc/sc, rep from * around (8dc/8sc).

**Shape top of neck:**

**Row 1:** 1ch, 1dc/1sc in each of next 4dc/4sc, turn.

Rep last row once more, ending with sl st in next dc/sc. Fasten off.

Sew up finishing row at back of neck by folding last 4dc/4sc in half and sewing

together. Stuff the head, avoiding the tip of the nose. Flatten the tip of the nose with your finger and use the tail end on the foundation row to sew up the end with a few stitches. Weave in the end.

**Shape neck:**

**Rnd 1:** Join on yarn MC with a sl st in a dc/sc near seam, 1dc/1sc in each dc/sc and row-end edge around neck, join into ring with sl st in first dc/sc of rnd (9dc/9sc).

**Rnd 2:** 1dc/1sc in each of next 9dc/9sc. Rep last rnd 10 times more, stuffing the neck as you crochet.

**Rnd 13:** 1dc/1sc in each of next 4dc/4sc, 2dc/2sc in next dc/sc, 1dc/1sc in each of next 4dc/4sc (10dc/10sc).

**Rnd 14:** 1dc/1sc in each of next 10dc/10sc. Rep last rnd twice more.

**Rnd 17:** 1dc/1sc in each of next 4dc/4sc, 2dc/2sc in each of next 2dc/2sc, 1dc/1sc in each of next 4dc/4sc (12dc/12sc).

**Rnd 18:** 1dc/1sc in each of next 12d/12sc. Rep last rnd twice more.

**Rnd 21:** 1dc/1sc in each of next 4dc/4sc, 2dc/2sc in each of next 4dc/4sc, 1dc/1sc in each of next 4dc/4sc (16dc/16sc).

**Shape body:**

**Rnd 22:** *1dc/1sc in next dc/sc, 2dc/2sc in next dc/sc, rep from * around (24dc/24sc).

**Rnd 23:** *1dc/1sc in each of next 2dc/2sc, 2dc/2sc in next dc/sc, rep from * around (32dc/32sc).

**Rnd 24:** 1dc/1sc in each of next 32dc/32sc.

Rep last rnd 9 times more.

**Shape bottom:**

**Rnd 34:** *1dc/1sc in each of next 7dc/7sc, miss next dc/sc, rep from * around

(28dc/28sc).

**Rnd 35:** 1dc/1sc in each of next 28dc/28sc.

**Rnd 36:** *1dc/1sc in each of next 6dc/6sc, miss next dc/sc, rep from * around (24dc/24sc).

**Rnd 37:** 1dc/1sc in each of next 24dc/24sc.

**Rnd 38:** *1dc/1sc in each of next 5dc/5sc, miss next dc/sc, rep from * around (20dc/20sc).

**Rnd 39:** 1dc/1sc in each of next 20dc/20sc.

**Rnd 40:** *1dc/1sc in each of next 4dc/4sc, miss next dc/sc, rep from * around (16dc/16sc).

**Rnd 41:** *1dc/1sc in each of next 3dc/3sc, miss next dc/sc, rep from * around (12dc/12sc).

Stuff the body.

**Rnd 42:** *1dc/1sc in each of next 2dc/2sc, miss next dc/sc, rep from * around (8dc/8sc).

**Rnd 43:** *1dc/1sc in next dc/sc, miss next dc/sc, rep from * around until the ring is closed.

Fasten off and weave in the end.

**EARS (make 2)**

**Foundation row:** Beg at the base of the ear where it joins the head, using yarn MC and 4.00mm (G-6) hook, make 2ch.

**Rnd 1:** 6dc/6sc in 2nd ch from hook.

**Rnd 2:** [1dc/1sc in next dc/sc, 2dc/2sc in next dc/sc] 3 times (9dc/9sc).

**Rnd 3:** 1dc/1sc in each of next 9dc/9sc, turn. Now work in rows.

**Row 1:** 1ch, 1dc/1sc in each of next 8dc/8sc, turn (8dc/8sc).

**Row 2:** Sl st in first dc/sc, 1ch, 1dc/1sc in each dc/sc across, turn (7dc/7sc).

Rep last row 6 times more.

**Rim of ear:**

**Next rnd:** Work in dc/sc evenly from the point around edge of ear and back to the point, sl st in first dc/sc.

Fasten off.

## HORNS (make 2)

**Foundation row:** Beg at top of horn, using yarn MC and 4.00mm (G-6) hook, make 2ch.

**Rnd 1:** 3dc/3sc in 2nd chain from hook, sl st in first top of first dc/sc, make 9ch. Fasten off, leaving a tail end with which to sew on the head.

## SMALL SPOTS (make 2)

**Foundation row:** Using yarn A and 4.00mm (G-6) hook, make 4ch, join with sl st in first ch to form ring.

**Rnd 1:** Working over loose end, 1ch, 8dc/8sc into ring (8dc/8sc).

**Rnd 2:** [1dc/1sc in next dc/sc, 2dc/2sc in next dc/sc] 4 times, sl st in top of first dc/sc (12dc/12sc).**

Fasten off. Pull up the centre tail end to close the ring, sew onto the neck with the other tail end.

## BIG SPOTS (make 2)

Work as for 'Small Spots' up to ** (12dc/12sc).

**Rnd 3:** [1dc/1sc in each of next 2dc/2sc, 2dc/2sc in next dc/sc] 4 times, sl st in top of first dc/sc (16dc/16sc).

Fasten off. Pull up the centre tail end to close the ring, sew onto the neck and body with the other tail end.

## HOOVES (make 4)

**Foundation row:** Using yarn B and 4.00mm (G-6) hook, make 2ch.

**Rnd 1:** 8dc/8sc in 2nd ch from hook.

**Rnd 2:** 2dc/2sc in each of next 8dc/8sc (16dc/16sc).

**Rnd 3:** 1dc/1sc in each of next 16dc/16sc. Rep last rnd 5 times more.

**Rnd 9:** [1dc/1sc in next dc/sc, miss next dc/sc] 8 times, sl st in top of first dc/sc (8dc/8sc). Fasten off.

## HIND LEGS (make 2)

**Foundation row:** Using yarn A and

4.00mm (G-6) hook, make 28ch.
**Row 1:** 1dc/1sc in 2nd ch from hook, 1dc/1sc in each ch across, turn.
**Rnd 2:** 1ch, 1dc/1sc in each dc/sc across, turn.
Rep last row twice more.
Fasten off. **

## FORELEGS (make 2)
**Foundation row:** Using yarn MC and 5.00mm (H-8) hook, make 28ch.
Make as for hind legs from ** to **.

## TAIL
**Foundation row:** Using yarn MC and 4.00mm (G-6) hook, make 10ch.
Fasten off.
Cut short lengths of yarn B and sew to one end of tail to create a fringe.

## TO FINISH
Using yarn MC, stitch a French knot at either side of the head, then sew a bead under each knot to make the eyes. Using black sewing thread used double, sew a fan of short stitches above the French knot as eyelashes. Using brown embroidery thread or yarn, sew two straight stitches to the nose for nostrils. Using pink embroidery thread or yarn, sew a stem stitch mouth under the nose.

Sew the ear base to the back/side of the head, then sew the horns to the top of the head. Sew the chin to the neck to pull the head down slightly. Sew up the back seam of each leg. Stuff each hoof, insert the legs just into the open end of the hoof and sew in place. The legs may need pressing to stop them from curling, but check the yarn manufacturer's guidelines before doing so. Sew on the tail. Tie the ribbon in a bow around one horn.

# Gown and scarf

## MATERIALS
One 50g ball of DK-weight (light worsted) cotton and acrylic blend in watermelon pink (MC)
One 50g ball of DK-weight (light worsted) metallic yarn in pewter (A)
One 50g ball of DK-weight (light worsted) nylon yarn with 'eyelash' or fluffy texture in magenta (B)
5.00mm (H-8) hook
Yarn needle

## TENSION (GAUGE)
13 sts and 12 rows to 5cm (2in) using yarn MC over dc/sc.

## GOWN

(Back and front worked in one piece)
**Foundation row:** Beg at the hem edge, using yarn MC, make 49ch.
**Row 1:** 1dc/1sc in 2nd ch from hook, 1dc/1sc in each ch across, turn (48dc/48sc).
**Row 2:** 1ch, 1dc/1sc in each dc/sc across, turn.
Rep last row 3 times more.
Fasten off yarn MC, join in yarn A and rep last row 5 times more.
Fasten off yarn A, join in yarn MC and rep last row 5 times more.
Fasten off yarn MC, join in yarn A and rep last row 5 times more.
Fasten off yarn A, join in yarn MC and cont as follows:
**Row 21:** 1ch, *1dc/1sc in each of next 3dc/3sc, miss next dc/sc, rep from * across, turn (36dc/36sc).
**Row 22:** 1ch, 1dc/1sc in each dc/sc across, turn (36dc/36sc).
Rep last row twice more.
**Row 25:** 1ch, *1dc/1sc in each of next 2dc/2sc, miss next dc/sc, rep from * across, turn (24dc/24sc).
**Row 26:** 1ch, [1dc/1sc in each of next 4dc/4sc, miss next 6dc/6sc, make 6ch] twice, 1dc/1sc in each of next 4dc/4sc. Fasten off.

## TO FINISH

Using MC yarn, sew up the back seam, weave in ends.

## SCARF

**Foundation row:** Using yarn B, make 35ch.
**Row 1:** 1dc/1sc in 2nd ch from hook, 1dc/1sc in each ch across (34dc/34sc).
**Row 2:** 1ch, 1dc/1sc in each dc/sc across. Fasten off.
Weave in ends.

# Larry the Lobster

**Bold and cheerful, this boisterous lobster looks as comfortable on rocky, muddy shorelines as he does in your child's warm embrace. This snazzy scavenger is deceptively cuddly!**

## SIZE
41cm (16in) long x 38cm (15in) wide (claws outstretched)

## MATERIALS
One 50g ball of super-chunky (super-bulky) wool in variegated lobster orange
Two 6mm (¼in) black glass beads or similar for eyes
10.00mm (N-15) hook
Polyester toy stuffing or wadding
Yarn needle

## TENSION (GAUGE)
9 sts and 8 rnds to 5cm (2in) over dc/sc.

## NOTE
Before beginning the second round in each section, place a marker or length of contrasting yarn across your crochet and up against the loop on the hook and above the working yarn. Work Rnd 2 then slip the marker out and place it at the beginning of the next round and so on. The marker will indicate where each subsequent round starts.

## BODY
**Foundation row:** Beg at tail, make 9ch.
**Row 1:** 1dc/1sc in 3rd ch from hook, 1dc/1sc in each of next 5ch, miss last ch, turn (6dc/6sc).
**Rows 2–4:** 1ch, 1dc/1sc in each dc/sc across, turn.
**Row 5:** Make 6ch, miss first 5dc/5sc, sl st in last dc/sc (12 sts).
Cont to work in rnds.
**Rnd 1:** 1dc/1sc in top of each of next 6dc/6sc, 1dc/1sc in each of next 6ch (12dc/12sc).
**Rnd 2:** 1dc/1sc in each dc/sc around. Rep last rnd once more.
**Rnd 4:** 1dc/1sc in top of each dc/sc around. Rep last 3 rnds twice more.
**Shape thorax:**
**Rnd 11:** *1dc/1sc in each of next 2dc/2sc, 2dc/2sc in next dc, rep from * around (16dc/16sc).

little, then the body and the head.

**Rnd 21:** *1dc/1sc in next dc/sc, miss next dc/sc, rep from * until gap is closed. Fasten off.

## CLAWS (make 2)

**Foundation row:** Beg at the body end, make 2ch.

**Rnd 1:** 6dc/6sc in 2nd ch from hook.

**Rnds 2 and 3:** 1dc/1sc in each of next 6dc/6sc.

**Rnd 4:** *1dc/1sc in next dc/sc, 2dc/2sc in next dc/sc, rep from * around (9dc/9sc).

**Rnd 5:** *1dc/1sc in each of next 2dc/2sc, 2dc/2sc in next dc/sc, rep from * around (12dc/12sc).

**Rnd 6:** *1dc/1sc in next dc/sc, miss next dc/sc, rep from * around (6dc/6sc).

**Shape large claw:**

**Rnd 7:** *1dc/1sc in next dc/sc, 2dc/2sc in next dc/sc, rep from * around (9dc/9sc).

**Rnd 8:** 1dc/1sc in each of next 4dc/4sc, 2dc/2sc in next dc/sc, 1dc/1sc in each of next 4dc/4sc (10dc/10sc).

**Rnd 9:** 1dc/1sc in each of next 4dc/4sc, 2dc/2sc in each of next 2dc/2sc, 1dc/1sc in each of next 4dc/4sc (12dc/12sc).

**Rnd 10:** 1dc/1sc in each of next 4dc/4sc, 2dc/2sc in each of next 4dc/4sc, 1dc/1sc in each of next 4dc/4sc (16dc/16sc).

**Rnd 11:** 1dc/1sc in each of next 16dc/16sc.

**Rnd 12:** 1dc/1sc in each dc/sc around.

Rep last rnd twice more.

**Rnd 15:** *1dc/1sc in each of next 3dc/3sc, miss next dc/sc, rep from * around (12dc/12sc).

**Rnd 16:** 1dc/1sc in each of next dc/sc around.

Rep last rnd twice more.

**Shape head:**

**Rnd 19:** *1dc/1sc in each of next 2dc/2sc, miss next dc/sc, rep from * around (8dc/8sc).

**Rnd 20:** [1dc/1sc in each of next 3dc/3sc, miss next dc/sc] twice (6dc/6sc).

Carefully turn out to other side, sew the edge of the abdomen at Rnd 1 to join with the top of the tail. Stuff the tail a

**Rnd 12:** *1dc/1sc in each of next 3dc/3sc, miss next dc/sc, rep from * around (12dc/12sc).

**Rnd 13:** *1dc/1sc in each of next 2dc/2sc, miss next dc/sc, rep from * around (8dc/8sc).

**Rnd 14:** 1dc/1sc in each of next 8dc/8sc.

**Shape large claw:**

**Rnd 15:** 1dc/1sc in each of next 8dc/8sc, turn.

Cont to work in rows.

**Row 1:** 1ch, 1dc/1sc in each of next 5dc/5sc, turn.

Rep last row once more.

**Row 3:** Sl st in first dc/sc, 1ch, 1dc/1sc in each of next 2dc/2sc, miss next dc/sc, 1dc/1sc in last dc/sc, turn (3dc/3sc).

**Row 4:** Sl st in first dc/sc, 1ch, 1dc/1sc in next dc/sc (1dc/1sc).

Fasten off.

## SMALL CLAW

**Foundation row:** Beg at the body end, make 6ch.

**Row 1:** 1dc/1sc in 2nd ch from hook, 1dc/1sc in each ch across, turn (5dc/5sc).

**Row 2:** Sl st in first dc, 1ch, 1dc/1sc in each of next 2dc/2sc, miss next dc/sc, 1dc/1sc in last dc/sc, turn (3dc/3sc).

**Row 3:** Sl st in first dc/sc, 1ch, miss next dc/sc, 1dc/1sc in last dc/sc, turn

(1dc/1sc).

**Row 4:** 1ch, 1dc/1sc in next dc/sc.

Fasten off.

## LEGS (make 8)

**Foundation row:** Beg at the body end, make 10ch. Fasten off.

Snip one tail end to about 2cm (¾in); use the other to sew onto the body.

## TO FINISH

For the rings around the tail, make three lengths of 16ch. Sew each chain around the tail along where rounds have been worked into top of dc/sc only. Cut two 30cm (12in) lengths of yarn for the antennae and sew to front of face. Sew the eyes just above these. Sew up the large pincers along row ends, leaving a small gap for stuffing each claw. Stuff the first part of the claws, leaving pincers unstuffed. Close gaps and shape pincers to a point. Sew the claws to the body near the eyes. Sew the legs, four on each side of the body, three pairs toward the head and last pair just above where the tail meets the body. Fold each small pincer in half widthways across the foundation row, sew up along row ends and lightly shape into a point. Sew a small pincer to the top of each claw.

# Sir Waldorf Walrus

**Even though he's a softie, such a grand, formidable creature deserves a title of honour. Waldorf will quickly become a firm favourite among little ones. With his long tusks and soft belly, this creature of the deep makes an intriguing and fun playmate.**

## SIZE
34cm (13½in) long

## MATERIALS
One 50g ball of aran-weight (worsted) wool and acrylic blend in grey-brown for head and body (MC)
One 50g ball of aran-weight (worsted) wool and acrylic blend in cream for cheeks and front fins (A)
Small amount of DK–weight (light worsted) wool in cream for tusks (B)
5.00mm (H-8) and 6.50mm (K-10½) hooks
Two 5mm (³⁄₁₆in) buttons for eyes
Brown yarn for nose
Black sewing thread for whiskers and for attaching buttons
Polyester toy stuffing or wadding
Yarn needle

## TENSION (GAUGE)
7 sts and 6½ rows to 5cm (2in) using 6.50mm (K-10½) hook and yarn MC over dc/sc.

## NOTE
Before beginning the second round in each section, place a marker or short length of contrasting yarn across your crochet and up against the loop on the hook and above the working yarn. Work Rnd 2, then slip the marker out and place it at the beginning of the next round and so on. The marker will indicate where each subsequent round starts.

## HEAD AND BODY
**Foundation row:** Beg at the head, using yarn MC and 6.50mm (K-10½) hook, make 2ch.
**Rnd 1:** 6dc/6sc in 2nd ch from hook.
**Rnd 2:** 2dc/2sc in each of next 6dc/6sc (12dc/12sc).
**Rnd 3:** *1dc/1sc in next dc/sc, 2dc/2sc in next dc/sc, rep from * around

(18dc/18sc).

**Rnd 4:** *1dc/1sc in each of next 2dc/2sc, 2dc/2sc in next dc/sc, rep from * around (24dc/24sc).

**Rnd 5:** 1dc/1sc in each dc/sc around. Rep last rnd 5 times more.

**Shape body:**

**Rnd 11:** 2dc/2sc in each of next 12dc/12sc, [1dc/1sc in next dc/sc, miss next dc/sc] 6 times (30dc/30sc).

**Rnd 12:** 1dc/1sc in each dc/sc around.

Rep last rnd 5 times more.

**Rnd 18:** 2dc/2sc in each of next 18dc/18sc, [1dc/1sc in next dc/sc, miss next dc/sc] 6 times (42dc/42sc).

**Rnd 19:** 1dc/1sc in each dc/sc around. Rep last rnd 5 times more.

**Rnd 25:** *1dc/1sc in each of next 2dc/2sc, miss next dc/sc, rep from * around (28dc/28sc).

**Rnd 26:** 1dc/1sc in each dc/sc around.

**Rnd 27:** *1dc/1sc in each of next 6dc/6sc,

miss next dc/sc, rep from * around (24dc/24sc).

**Rnd 28:** 1dc/1sc in each dc/sc around.

**Rnd 29:** *1dc/1sc in each of next 5dc/5sc, miss next dc/sc, rep from * around (20dc/20sc).

Stuff the walrus up to this row, then cont as follows:

**Rnd 30:** 1dc/1sc in each dc/sc around.

**Rnd 31:** *1dc/1sc in each of next 4dc/4sc, miss next dc/sc, rep from * around (16dc/16sc).

**Rnd 32:** 1dc/1sc in each dc/sc around.

**Rnd 33:** *1dc/1sc in each of next 3dc/3sc, miss next dc/sc, rep from * around (12dc/12sc).

**Rnd 34:** 1dc/1sc in each dc/sc around.

**Rnd 35:** *1dc/1sc in each of next 4dc/4sc, miss next dc/sc, rep from * around (6dc/6sc).

**Rnd 36:** 1dc/1sc in each dc/sc around. Rep last rnd 5 times more.

Stuff the last of the body.

**Rnd 42:** *1dc/1sc in next dc/sc, miss next dc/sc, rep from * around until the ring is closed.

Fasten off.

## CHEEKS (make 2)

**Foundation row:** Beg at the head, using yarn A and 5.00mm (H-8) hook, make 2ch.

**Rnd 1:** 6dc/6sc in 2nd ch from hook.

**Rnd 2:** 2dc/2sc in each of next 6dc/6sc (12dc/12sc).

**Rnd 3:** 1dc/1sc in each dc/sc around.

**Rnd 4:** *1dc/1sc in next dc/sc, 2dc/2sc in next dc/sc, rep from * around (18dc/18sc).

**Rnd 5:** 1dc/1sc in each dc/sc around.

**Rnd 6:** *1dc/1sc in next dc/sc, miss next dc/sc, rep from * around (9dc/9sc).

Stuff with a matching yarn to pad out.

**Rnd 7:** *1dc/1sc in next dc/sc, miss next dc/sc, rep from * until the ring is closed.

Fasten off.

## FRONT FINS (make 2)

**Foundation row:** Using yarn A and 5.00mm (H-8) hook, beg at the part of fin that is later sewn to body, make 8ch.

**Row 1:** 1dc/1sc in 2nd ch from hook, 1dc/1sc in each ch across, turn (7dc/7sc).

**Row 2:** 1ch, 1dc/1sc in each dc/sc across, turn.

**Row 3:** 2ch, 1tr/1dc in each dc/sc across, turn.

**Row 4:** 2ch, 1htr/1hdc in each of next 4tr/4dc, 1dc/1sc in each of next 3tr/3dc, turn.

**Row 5:** 1ch, 1dc/1sc in each of next 3dc/3sc, 1htr/1hdc in each of next 4htr/4hdc, turn.

**Row 6:** 2ch, 1htr/1hdc in each of next 4htr/4hdc, 1dc/1sc in each of next 3dc/3sc.
Fasten off.

## TAIL FINS (make 2)

**Foundation row:** Using yarn MC and 5.00mm (H-8) hook, beg at the part of fin that is later sewn to body, make 5ch.
**Row 1:** 1dc/1sc in 2nd ch from hook, 1dc/1sc in each ch across, turn (4dc/4sc).
**Row 2:** 1ch, 1dc/1sc in each dc/sc across, turn.
**Row 3:** 2ch, 1tr/1dc in next dc/sc, 1htr/1hdc in next dc/sc, 1dc/1sc in each of next 2dc/2sc.
Fasten off.

## TUSKS (make 2)

**Foundation row:** Using yarn B and 5.00mm (H-8) hook, beg at the part of fin that is later sewn to body, make 13ch.
**Row 1:** 1dc/1sc in 2nd ch from hook, 1dc/1sc in each ch across.
Fasten off, leaving the tail ends.

## TO FINISH

Using matching yarn, sew the front fins onto each side of the body, curving the fin slightly as you stitch so that you sew in an arc shape. Sew the two tail fins at either side at the end of the tail. Sew the cheeks onto the front of the head, then sew these together where they meet. Using brown yarn, oversew nose, catching the cheeks on each side. Using black thread, sew a few loose running stitches on each cheek to form whiskers.

Sew on the two button eyes at either side of the head. Sew on the tusks under the cheeks, using the tail ends. You may wish to press these with a cool iron if they curl a little, but check the yarn manufacturer's guidelines first.

Pinch the middle of the back to pull up the walrus's back a little. Then, using matching yarn, sew a few discreet stitches to hold in place.

# Horse and Foal

Mama Horse is a glove puppet, and her young foal is a delightful toy. They can cuddle together when it's time for a tea party or a bedtime story.

## Horse

### SIZE
33 x 12cm (13 x 4¾in)

### MATERIALS
Two 50g balls of DK-weight (light worsted) merino in gold (MC)
Small amount of DK-weight (light worsted) alpaca in brown for muzzle (A)
One 50g ball of DK-weight (light worsted) acrylic in lilac for mane (B)
4.00mm (G-6) hook
Small pieces of felt in three colours for inner and outer eyes and for nose
Thread for attaching felt and beads
Two 6mm (¼in) black glass beads or similar for eyes
Dark brown yarn for mouth
Two dressmaker's pins
Yarn needle

### TENSION (GAUGE)
9 sts and 10 rows to 5cm (2in) using yarn MC over dc/sc.

### NOTE
Before beginning the second round in each section, place a marker or short length of contrasting yarn across your crochet and up against the loop on the hook and above the working yarn. Work Rnd 2, then slip the marker out and place it at the beginning of the next round and so on. The marker will indicate where each subsequent round starts.

### HEAD & BODY
Using yarn A, beg at the muzzle end, make 3ch.
**Foundation rnd:** Working over tail end, 8dc/8sc in 3rd ch from hook, join to top of 3ch with sl st to form ring (8dc/8sc).
**Rnd 1:** 1dc/1sc in each of next 8dc/8sc.
**Rnd 2:** 2dc/2sc in each of next 8dc/8sc (16dc/16sc).
**Rnd 3:** 1dc/1sc in each of next 16dc/16sc.
**Rnd 4:** *1dc/1sc in next dc/sc, 2dc/2sc in next dc/sc, rep from * around (24dc/24sc).
**Rnd 5:** 1dc/1sc in each of next 24dc/24sc, sl st in top of first dc/sc.

## Shape muzzle:

**Rnd 6:** 1ch, 1dc/1sc in same place as sl st was worked, 1dc/1sc in each of next 24dc/24sc (25dc/25sc).

**Rnd 7:** Miss the sl st and the 1ch, work 1dc/1sc into top of first dc/sc of previous rnd, 1dc/1sc into each of rem 24dc/24sc (25dc/25sc).

**Rnd 8:** Change to yarn MC, 1tr/1dc in each of next 25dc/25sc, at the same time catching in the marker.

**Rnd 9:** 1tr/1dc in each of next 24tr/24dc, 2tr/2dc in last tr/dc (26tr/26dc).

**Rnd 10:** 1tr/1dc in each of next 26tr/26dc.

**Rnd 11:** 1tr/1dc in each of next 25tr/25dc, 2tr/2dc in last tr/dc (27tr/26dc).

**Rnd 12:** 1tr/1dc in each of next 27tr/27dc.

**Rnd 13:** 1tr/1dc in each of next 26tr/26dc, 2tr/2dc in last tr/dc (28tr/28dc).

**Rnd 14:** 1tr/1dc in each of next 28tr/28dc.

**Rnd 15:** 1tr/1dc in each of next 27tr/27dc, 2tr/2dc in last tr/dc, sl st to top of first tr/dc of rnd (29tr/29dc).

## Shape chin:

**Row 1:** 2ch (counts as 1tr/1dc), miss tr/dc where sl st was worked, miss next tr/dc, 1tr/dc in each of next 24tr/24dc, miss next tr/dc, 1tr/1dc in next tr/dc, turn (26tr/26dc).

**Row 2:** 2ch (counts as 1tr/1dc), miss first 2tr/2dc, 1tr/1dc in each of next 23tr/23dc, 1tr/1dc in top of 2ch at beg of previous row, turn (25tr/25dc).

**Row 3:** 2ch (counts as 1tr/1dc), miss first 2tr/2dc, 1tr/1dc in each of next 22tr/22dc, 1tr/1dc in top of 2ch at beg of previous row, turn (24tr/24dc).

**Row 4:** 2ch (counts as 1tr/1dc), miss first 2tr/2dc, 1tr/1dc in each of next 21tr/21dc, 1tr/1dc in top of 2ch at beg of previous row, turn (23tr/23dc).

**Row 5:** 2ch (counts as 1tr/1dc), miss first tr/dc, 1tr/1dc in each of next 20tr/20dc, 2tr/2dc in next tr/dc, 1tr/1dc in top of 2ch at beg of previous row, join with sl st in top of 2ch at beg of row (24tr/24dc). Cont to work in spiral rnds (do not turn and keep with RS facing), placing marker at the beg of each rnd for 15 rnds, at the same time increasing 2 sts on every third rnd as follows:

**Rnd 3:** 1tr/1dc in each of next 11tr/11dc, 2tr/2dc in next tr/dc, 1tr/1dc in each of next 11tr/11dc, 2tr/2dc in last tr/dc (26tr/26dc).

**Rnd 6:** 1tr/1dc in each of next 12tr/12dc, 2tr/2dc in next tr/dc, 1tr/1dc in each of next 12tr/12dc, 2tr/2dc in last tr/dc (28tr/28dc).

**Rnd 9:** 1tr/1dc in each of next 13tr/13dc, 2tr/2dc in next tr/dc, 1tr/1dc in each of next 13tr/13dc, 2tr/2dc in last tr/dc

(30tr/30dc).
Cont increasing as above until there are
34tr/34dc.
Fasten off.

## EARS (make 2)
Using 2 strands of yarn MC and A
together, make 3ch.
**Foundation rnd:** Working over tail end,
8dc/8sc in third ch from hook, join to top
of 3ch with sl st to form ring.
**Rnd 1:** 1dc/1sc in each of next 8dc/8sc.
**Rnd 2:** 2dc/2sc in each of next 8dc/8sc
(16dc/16sc).
**Rnd 3:** 1dc/1sc in each of next 15dc/15sc,
2dc/2sc in next dc/sc (17dc/17sc).
**Rnd 4:** 1dc/1sc in each of next 17dc/17sc.
Drop yarn A and cont with yarn MC for
the following rows:
**Next row:** 1dc/1sc in each of next
15dc/15sc, turn.
**Next row:** 1ch, miss first dc/sc, 1dc/1sc
in each of next 11dc/11sc, miss next dc/sc,
1dc/1sc in next dc/sc, turn (13dc/13sc).
Rep last row 6 times more, working
2dc/2sc less before last dc/sc on every
row (1dc/1sc).
Fasten off.

## TO FINISH
With RS facing, using a blunt-ended
yarn needle and matching yarn,
backstitch the chin seam.

To mark where to sew on the ears, place
the puppet over your hand (seam facing
down), carefully pin two dressmaker's
pins onto the crochet at the position
where your wrist bends – the ears should
lie 2.5cm (1in) apart with the inner ears
facing outwards. Carefully take off the
puppet and sew the ears in place, with
matching yarn, around the first row of
dc/sc stitches.

Referring to the photograph as a guide,
cut out two irises, two pupils and two
nostrils from coloured felt. Join each
pupil to its iris by sewing a glass bead to
the centre.

Referring to the photograph, sew on
the felt nostrils and eyes with small
stitches around the outer edges, taking
care to sew through only one layer on
the horse's nose. Using a short length
of dark brown yarn, stem stitch a line
across the nose to create the mouth.

To attach the mane, cut lengths of
yarn B to about 10cm (4in). Taking two
lengths at a time, bend both in half.

Use a crochet hook to pull the loop through a tr/dc stitch at the top of the head between the ears. Pass the cut ends through the loops, then pull the cut ends so that the knot lies at the top of the head. Continue with this fringing technique along the top of the head and a little way down the back of the neck.

# Foal

## SIZE
26 x 26cm (10¼ x 10¼in)

## MATERIALS
Two 50g balls of DK-weight (light worsted) wool and acrylic blend in buttercup yellow for head and body (MC)
Small amount of DK-weight (light worsted) acrylic in lilac for mane and tail (A)
Small amount of DK-weight (light worsted angora and acrylic blend in brown for hooves (B)
4.00mm (G-6) and 5.00mm (H-8) hooks
Small pieces of felt in three colours for inner and outer eyes and for nostrils
Thread for attaching felt and beads
Two 6mm (¼in) black glass beads or similar for eyes
Pink yarn for mouth
Polyester toy stuffing or wadding
Yarn needle

## TENSION (GAUGE)
12 sts and 9 rnds to 5cm (2in) using yarn MC and 5.00mm (H-8) hook over dc/sc.

## HEAD & BODY
Using yarn A and 5.00mm (H-8) hook, beg at the muzzle end, make 3ch.
**Foundation rnd:** Working over tail end, 8dc/8sc in third ch from hook, join to top of 3ch with sl st to form ring (8dc/8sc).
**Rnd 1:** 1dc/1sc in each of next 8dc/8sc.
**Rnd 2:** 2dc/2sc in each of next 8dc/8sc (16dc/16sc).
**Rnd 3:** 1dc/1sc in each of next 16dc/16sc. Rep last rnd three times more, ending with sl st in top of first dc/sc of rnd.
**Rnd 7:** Join in yarn MC to same place as sl st was worked, 1dc/1sc in each of next 16dc/16sc.
**Shape nose:**
**Rnd 8:** 2dc/2sc in each of next 6dc/6sc, 1dc/1sc in each of next 10dc/10sc (22dc/22sc).
**Rnd 9:** 1dc/1sc in each of next 22dc/22sc. Rep last rnd 4 times more.
**Rnd 14:** [1dc/1sc in next dc/sc, miss dc/sc] 6 times, 1dc/1sc in each of next

10dc/10sc (16dc/16sc).

**Rnd 15:** 1dc/1sc in each dc/sc around.

**Shape chin:**

**Rnd 16:** [1dc/1sc in each of next 2dc/2sc, miss next dc/sc] 5 times, 1dc/1sc in next dc/sc (11dc/11sc).

**Rnd 17:** 1dc/1sc in each dc/sc around. Rep last rnd once more.

**Shape neck:**

**Rnd 19:** [1dc/1sc in each of next 3dc/3sc, 2dc/2sc in next dc/sc] twice, 1dc/1sc in each of next 3dc/3sc (13dc/13sc).

**Rnd 20:** 1dc/1sc in each dc/sc around.

**Rnd 21:** [1dc/1sc in each of next 3dc/3sc, 2dc/2sc in next dc/sc] 3 times, 1dc/1sc in next dc/sc (16dc/16sc).

**Rnd 22:** 1dc/1sc in each dc/sc around.

**Rnd 23:** [1dc/1sc in each of next 3dc/3sc, 2dc/2sc in next dc/sc] 4 times (20dc/20sc).

**Rnd 24:** 1dc/1sc in each dc/sc around. Rep last rnd 3 times more.

**Rnd 28:** 1dc/1sc in each of next 5dc/5sc, [1dc/1sc in each of next 2dc/2sc, 2dc/2sc in next dc/sc] 4 times, 1dc/1sc in each of next 3dc/3sc (24dc/24sc).

**Rnd 29:** 1dc/1sc in each dc/sc around. Rep last rnd 3 times more.

**Body shaping:**

**Rnd 33:** 1dc/1sc in each of next 8dc/8sc, 2dc/2sc in each of next 7dc/7sc, 1dc/1sc in each of next 9dc/9sc (31dc/31sc).

**Rnd 34:** 1dc/1sc in each dc/sc around.

**Rnd 35:** 1dc/1sc in each of next 10dc/10sc, 2dc/2sc in each of next 11dc/11sc, 1dc/1sc in each of next 10dc/10sc (42dc/42sc).

**Rnd 36:** 1dc/1sc in each dc/sc around. Rep last rnd 4 times more.

**Rnd 41:** 1dc/1sc in each of next 11dc/11sc, [miss next dc/sc, 1dc/1sc in next dc/sc] 10 times, 1dc/1sc in each of next 11dc/11sc (32dc/32sc).

**Rnd 42:** 1dc/1sc in each dc/sc around.

**Shape back:**

**Rnd 43:** [Miss next dc/sc, 1dc/1sc in each of next 3dc/3sc] twice, 1dc/1sc in each of next 16dc/16sc, [miss next dc/sc, 1dc/1sc in each of next 3dc/3sc] twice (28dc/28sc).

**Rnd 44:** 1dc/1sc in each dc/sc around.

**Rnd 45:** [Miss next dc/sc, 1dc/1sc in each of next 3dc/3sc] twice, 1dc/1sc in each of next 12dc/12sc, [miss next dc/sc, 1dc/1sc in each of next 3dc/3sc] twice (24dc/24sc).

**Rnd 46:** 1dc/1sc in each dc/sc around. Rep last rnd 3 times more.

**Shape hips:**

**Rnd 50:** [1dc/1sc in each of next 2dc/2sc, 2dc/2sc in next dc/sc] 8 times (32dc/32sc).

**Rnd 51:** [1dc/1sc in next dc/sc, 2dc/2sc in next dc/sc] 16 times (48dc/48sc).

**Rnd 52:** 2dc/2sc in each of next 10dc/10sc, 1dc/1sc in each of next 28dc/28sc, 2dc/2sc in each of next 10dc/10sc (68dc/68sc).

**Rnd 53:** 1dc/1sc in each dc/sc around. Rep last rnd 4 times more.

**Rnd 58:** *1dc/1sc in next dc/sc, miss next dc/sc, rep from * around (34dc/34sc). Rep last rnd once more (17dc/17sc). Stuff head and body.

**Rnd 60:** Sl st every other stitch around until opening is closed.

## EARS (make 2)

Using yarn MC and 4.00mm (G-6) hook, make 3ch.

**Foundation rnd:** Working over tail end, 8dc/8sc in third ch from hook, join to top of 3ch with sl st to form ring.

**Rnd 1:** 1dc/1sc in each of next 8dc/8sc.

**Next row:** 1dc/1sc in each of next 6dc/6sc, turn.

**Next row:** 1ch, 1dc/1sc in each of next 6dc/6sc, turn.

**Next row:** 1ch, miss first dc/sc, 1dc/1sc in each of next 3dc/3sc, miss 1dc/1sc, 1dc/1sc in last dc/sc, turn (4dc/4sc).

**Next row:** 1ch, miss first dc/sc, 1dc/1sc in next dc/sc, miss next dc/sc, 1dc/1sc in last dc/sc, turn (2dc/2sc).

**Next row:** Miss first dc/sc, sl st in last dc/sc.
Fasten off. Turn ear inside out.

## LEGS (make 4)

Beg with the hoof, using yarn B and 5.00mm (H-8) hook, make 3ch.

**Foundation rnd:** Working over tail end, 8dc/8sc in third ch from hook, join to top of 3ch with sl st to form ring.

**Rnd 1:** 2dc/2sc in each of next 8dc/8sc (16dc/16sc).

**Rnd 2:** 1dc/1sc in each of next 16dc/16sc. Rep last rnd twice more.

**Shape front of hoof:**

**Rnd 5:** Miss first 2dc/2sc, 1dc/1sc in each of next 14dc/14sc (14dc/14sc).

**Rnd 6:** Miss first 2dc/2sc, 1dc/1sc in each of next 12dc/12sc, sl st to first dc/sc (12dc/12sc).
Break off yarn B.

**Rnd 7:** Join in yarn MC (leg colour) to same place as sl st was worked, 1dc/1sc in each of next 12dc/12sc, sl st to first dc/sc.

**Rnd 8:** 1dc/1sc in each of next 12dc/12sc.

**Shape hoof:**

**Rnd 9:** [1dc /1sc in next dc/sc, miss next dc/sc] 6 times (6dc/6sc).
Stuff hoof.

**Rnd 10:** 1dc/1sc in each of next 6dc/6sc. Rep last rnd 3 times more.

## Shape knees:

**Rnd 14:** [1dc/1sc in each of next 2dc/2sc, 2dc/2sc in next dc/sc] twice (8dc/8sc).

**Rnd 15:** [1dc/1sc in next dc/sc, 2dc/2sc in next dc/sc] 4 times (12dc/12sc).

**Rnd 16:** 1dc/1sc in each of next 12dc/12sc.

**Rnd 17:** [1dc/1sc in each of next 2dc/2sc, miss next dc/sc] 4 times (8dc/8sc).

**Rnd 18:** [1dc/1sc in each of next 3dc/3sc, miss next dc/sc] twice (6dc/6sc).

**Rnd 19:** 1dc/1sc in each of next 6dc/6sc.
Rep last rnd 5 times more.

## Shape top of leg:

**Rnd 25:** [1dc/1sc in next dc/sc, 2dc/2sc in next dc/sc] 3 times (9dc/9sc).

**Rnd 26:** 1dc/1sc in each of next 9dc/9sc.
Rep last rnd 3 times more.

**Rnd 30:** [1dc/1sc in each of next 2dc/2sc, miss next dc/sc] 3 times (6dc/6sc).
Stuff lightly.
Sl st every other stitch around until opening is closed.

## TO FINISH

Using a blunt-ended yarn needle and MC yarn, sew the four legs to the underside of the body equidistant to one another.

Sew the base of each ear in place, referring to the photograph for positioning, taking care not to sew the two sides of the head together.

Referring to the photograph as a guide, cut out two irises, two pupils and two nostrils from coloured felt. Join each pupil to its iris by sewing a glass bead to the centre. Referring to the photograph, sew on the felt nostrils and eyes with small stitches around the outer edges, taking care to sew through only one layer on the horse's nose. Using a short length of pink yarn, stem stitch a line across the nose to create the mouth.

To attach the mane, cut lengths of yarn to about 10cm (4in). Taking two lengths at a time, bend both in half. Use a crochet hook to pull the loop through a dc/sc stitch at the top of the head between the ears. Pass the cut ends through the loops, then pull the cut ends so that the knot lies at the top of the head. Continue with this fringing technique along the top of the head and a little way down the back of the neck.

To attach the tail, follow the instructions for attaching the mane and make the strands twice as long.

# Pig and Piglet

**No playpen would be complete without this floppy-eared pair! Plump piggies like this could only be stitched in chunky yarn.**

## SIZES
**Pig:** 42 x 22cm (16½ x 8¾in)
**Piglet:** 15 x 8cm (6 x 3in)

## MATERIALS
One 50g ball of chunky (bulky) wool in shell pink for pig's body (MC)
Small amount of aran-weight (worsted) wool and nylon blend in pink for ears (A)
Small amount of aran-weight (worsted) wool and nylon blend in chocolate for markings on legs (B)
One ball of DK-weight (light worsted) alpaca and merino blend in strawberry pink for piglet's body (C)
Small amount of DK-weight (light worsted) alpaca and merino blend in brown for spots (D)
Small amounts of grey, blue and cream yarn for eyes
Dark brown yarn for mouth
4.00mm (G-6), 6.50mm (K-10½) and 8.00mm (L-11) hooks
Polyester toy stuffing or wadding
Yarn needle

## TENSION (GAUGE)
7 sts and 6 rows to 5cm (2in) using 6.50mm (K-10½) hook and yarn MC over dc/sc.

## NOTE
Before beginning the second round in each section, place a marker or short length of contrasting yarn across your crochet and up against the loop on the hook and above the working yarn. Work Rnd 2, then slip the marker out and place it at the beginning of the next round and so on. The marker will indicate where each subsequent round starts.

# Pig

## HEAD & BODY
**Foundation row:** Using yarn MC and 8.00mm (L-11) hook, beg at the snout, make 2ch.
**Rnd 1:** 6dc/6sc in second ch from hook.
**Rnd 2:** 2dc/2sc in each of next 6dc/6sc (12dc/12sc).

**Rnd 3:** *1dc/1sc in next dc/sc, 2dc/2sc in next dc/sc, rep from * around (18dc/18sc).

**Rnd 4:** 1dc/1sc in each of next 18dc/18sc. Change to 6.50mm (K-10½) hook, rep last rnd 4 times more.

**Shape top of head:**

**Rnd 9:** 2dc/2sc in each of next 9dc/9sc, 1dc/1sc in each of next 9dc/9sc (27dc/27sc).

**Rnd 10:** [1dc/1sc in next dc/sc, 2dc/2sc in next dc/sc] 9 times, 1dc/1sc in each of next 9dc/9sc (36dc/36sc).

**Rnd 11:** 1dc/1sc in each of next 36dc/36sc.

**Shape chin:**

**Rnd 12:** 1dc/1sc in each of next 27dc/27sc, [2dc/2sc in next dc/sc, 1dc/1sc in next dc/sc] 4 times, 1dc/1sc in last dc/sc (40dc/40sc).

**Rnd 13:** 1dc/1sc in each of next 40dc/40sc.

Rep last rnd 3 times more.

**Shape head:**

**Rnd 17:** [1dc/1sc in each of next 4dc/4sc, miss next dc/sc, 1dc/1sc in each of next 3dc/3sc, miss next dc/sc] 4 times, 1dc/1sc in each of next 3dc/3sc, miss next dc/sc (31dc/31sc).

**Rnd 18:** [1dc/1sc in each of next 6dc/6sc, miss next dc/sc) 3 times, 1dc/1sc in each

of next 10dc/10sc (28dc/28sc). Change to 8.00mm (L-11) hook.

**Rnd 19:** 1dc/1sc in each of next 28dc/28sc.

Rep last rnd twice more.

**Rnd 22:** [1dc/1sc in each of next 2dc/2sc, miss next dc/sc] 6 times, 1dc/1sc in each of next 10dc/10sc (22dc/22sc).

**Rnd 23:** 1dc/1sc in each of next 4dc/4sc, 2dc/2sc in each of next 14dc/14sc, 1dc/1sc in each of next 4dc/4sc (36dc/36sc).

**Rnd 24:** 1dc/1sc in each of next 36dc/36sc.

Rep last rnd until the head and body measure 33cm (13in) from snout to back end.

Stuff the snout, head and body.

**Next rnd:** *1dc/1sc in each of next 2dc/2sc, miss next dc/sc, rep from * around until the gap closes.

Make 15ch for the tail, twist it to curl it a little, fasten off.

## LARGE SPOT

**Foundation row:** Using yarn D and 4.00mm (G-6) hook, make 2ch.

**Rnd 1:** 6dc/6sc in second ch from hook.

**Rnd 2:** 2dc/2sc in each of next 6dc/6sc (12dc/12sc).

**Rnd 3:** *1dc/1sc in next dc/sc, 2dc/2sc

in next dc/sc, rep from * around
(18dc/18sc).**
**Rnd 4:** *1dc/1sc in each of next 2dc/2sc,
2dc/2sc in next dc/sc, rep from * around
(24dc/24sc).
**Rnd 5:** *1dc/1sc in each of next 3dc/3sc,
2dc/2sc in next dc/sc, rep from * around
(30dc/30sc).
**Rnd 6:** *1dc/1sc in each of next 4dc/4sc,
2dc/2sc in next dc/sc, rep from * around,
ending with sl st in top of next dc/sc
(36dc/36sc).
Fasten off.

## SMALL SPOT

Work as for large spot up to **, ending
with sl st in top of next dc/sc.
Fasten off.

## EARS (make 2)

**Foundation row:** Using yarn A and
8.0mm (L-11) hook, beg at the top of the
ear, make 17ch.
**Row 1:** 1dc/1sc in second ch from hook,
1dc/1sc in each of next 12ch, miss next
ch, 1dc/1sc in last ch, turn (14dc/14sc).
**Row 2:** 1ch, miss first dc/sc, 1dc/1sc in
each of next 11dc/11sc, miss next dc/sc,
1dc/1sc in last dc/sc, turn (12dc/12sc).
**Row 3:** 1ch, miss first dc/sc, 1dc/1sc in
each of next 9dc/9sc, miss next dc/sc,

1dc/1sc in last dc/sc, turn (10dc/10sc).
**Row 4:** 1ch, miss first dc/sc, 1dc/1sc in
each of next 7dc/7sc, miss next dc/sc,
1dc/1sc in last dc/sc, turn (8dc/8sc).
**Row 5:** 1ch, miss first dc/sc, 1dc/1sc in
each of next 5dc/5sc, miss next dc/sc,
1dc/1sc in last dc/sc, turn (6dc/6sc).
**Row 6:** 1ch, miss first dc/sc, 1dc/1sc in
each of next 3dc/3sc, miss next dc/sc,
1dc/1sc in last dc/sc, turn (4dc/4sc).
Fasten off.

## HIND LEGS (make 2)

**Foundation row:** Using yarn MC and
6.50mm (K-10½) hook, beg at the base of
the trotter, make 2ch.
**Rnd 1:** 6dc/6sc in second ch from hook.
**Rnd 2:** 2dc/2sc in each of next 6dc/6sc
(12dc/12sc).
**Rnd 3:** 1dc/1sc in each of next 12dc/12sc,
sl st in top of first dc/sc (12dc/12sc).
Join in yarn B to same place as sl st was
worked.
**Rnd 4:** 1dtr/1tr in each of next 12dc/12sc
(12dtr/12tr).
**Rnd 5:** 1dtr/1tr in each of next 12dtr/12tr,
sl st in top of first dtr/tr.
**Rnd 6:** Join in yarn MC in same place as
sl st was worked, 1dc/1sc in each of next
12dtr/12tr (12dc/12sc).
**Rnd 7:** 1dc/1sc in each of next 12dc/12sc.

**Shape front of leg:**
**Rnd 8:** 1dc/1sc in each of next 3dc/3sc, [1dc/1sc in next dc/sc, 2dc/2sc in next dc/sc] 3 times, 1dc/1sc in each of next 3dc/3sc (15dc/15sc).**
**Rnd 9:** 1dc/1sc in each of next 4dc/4sc, 2dc/2sc in each of next 7dc/7sc, 1dc/1sc in each of next 4dc/4sc (22dc/22sc).
**Rnd 10:** 1dc/1sc in each of next 22dc/22sc. Rep last rnd twice more. Fasten off.

## FORELEGS (make 2)
Work as for hind leg up to **.
**Rnd 9:** 1dc/1sc in each of next 15dc/15sc. Rep last rnd once more. Fasten off.

## TO FINISH
Sew the ears in place with a decreasing row edge oversewn onto the top of the head. Around the top edge of the snout, between rows 2 and 4, sew a backstitch line to shape the rim of the snout. Sew four short rows of grey yarn together to create the eyes. Onto this, sew a French knot in a small length of cream yarn. Make 10ch in a short length of blue yarn and sew around the grey. Sew a mouth across the bottom of the snout using a length of dark brown yarn. Sew on the spots with WS facing up. Sew on the hind legs with front facing forward,

leaving a gap for stuffing. Stuff the legs, then sew up the gap. Sew on the forelegs with front facing you and stuff as before.

# Piglet

Make all in one piece.
**Foundation row:** Using yarn C and 4.00mm (G-6) hook, beg at the snout, make 4ch.
**Row 1:** 2dc/2sc in second ch from hook, 1dc/1sc in next ch, 2dc/2sc in last ch, turn (5dc/5sc).
**Row 2:** 1ch, 2dc/2sc in first dc/sc, 1dc/1sc in each dc/sc to last dc/sc, 2dc/2sc in last dc/sc, turn (7dc/7sc).
Rep last row 4 times more (15dc/15sc).
**Row 7:** 1ch, 1dc/1sc in each of next 15dc/15sc, make 7ch for first front leg, turn.
**Row 8:** 1dc/1sc in second ch from hook, 1dc/1sc in each of next 5ch, 1dc/1sc in each of next 15dc/15sc, make 7ch for second front leg, turn.
**Row 9:** 1dc/1sc in second ch from hook, 1dc/1sc in each of next 5ch, 1dc/1sc in each of next 21dc/21sc, turn (27dc/27sc).
**Row 10:** 1ch, 1dc/1sc in each of next 27dc/27sc, turn.
Rep last row twice more.
**Row 13:** 1ch, 1dc/1sc in each of next

21dc/21sc, turn.

**Row 14:** 1ch, 1dc/1sc in each of next 15dc/15sc, turn.

Rep last row 3 times more.

**Row 18:** 1ch, 1dc/1sc in each of next 15dc/15sc, make 7ch for first back leg, turn.

**Row 19:** 1dc/1sc in second ch from hook, 1dc/1sc in each of next 5ch, 1dc/1sc in each of next 15dc/15sc, make 7ch for second back leg, turn.

**Row 20:** 1dc/1sc in second ch from hook, 1dc/1sc in each of next 5ch, 1dc/1sc in each of next 21dc/21sc, turn (27dc/27sc).

**Row 21:** 1ch, 1dc/1sc in each of next 27dc/27sc, turn.

Rep last row twice more.

**Row 24:** 1ch, 1dc/1sc in each of next 21dc/21sc, turn.

**Row 25:** 1ch, 1dc/1sc in each of next 15dc/15sc. Fasten off.

## EARS (make 2)

**Foundation row:** Using yarn C and 4.00mm (G-6) hook, beg at the base of the ear, make 6ch.

**Row 1:** 1dc/1sc in second ch from hook, 1dc/1sc in each of next 4ch, turn (5dc/5sc).

**Row 2:** 1ch, 1dc/1sc in each of next 5dc/5sc, turn.

Rep last row twice more.

**Row 5:** 1ch, miss first dc/sc, 1dc/1sc in each of next 2dc/2sc, miss next dc/sc, 1dc/1sc in last dc/sc, turn (3dc/3sc).

**Row 6:** 1ch, 1dc/1sc in each of next 3dc/3sc, turn.

**Row 7:** 1ch, miss first 2dc/2sc, 1dc/1sc in last dc/sc. Fasten off.

## TO FINISH

With RS facing and using matching yarn and backstitch throughout, fold in half across short row ends, sew around each leg, turn the legs out. Place body and head RS facing, sew along the bottom. Sew along the snout and under the chin, up to first pair of legs. Turn out. Stuff the legs a little, stuff the head and body, sew up the belly.

Using yarn C, make 10ch, join into a ring with a sl st in first ch, fasten off. Sew onto the end of the snout.

Sew the ears in place with base edge sewn onto the top of the head.
Using yarn C, make 10ch, twist the length of crochet, fasten off. Sew one end onto the back of the piglet for the tail.

Using grey yarn, sew the eyes onto the head with straight stitches.

# Cow and Calf

**Moo-licious! These two make a lovely pair when out to pasture. Clover boasts a striking black-and-white pattern that's accented with pink. Her calf, still wobbly on all fours, makes a fine finger puppet.**

## SIZES
**Cow:** 19cm (7½in) long x 10cm (4in) wide
**Calf:** 11cm (4½in) long x 6.5cm (2½in) wide

## MATERIALS
One 50g ball of DK-weight (light worsted) wool and acrylic blend in black (A)
One 50g ball of DK-weight (light worsted) wool and acrylic blend in white (MC)
Small amount of DK-weight (light worsted) cotton yarn in light pink for nose and udder (B)
5.00mm (H-8) hook
Black sewing thread for attaching beads
Two 6mm (¼in) black glass beads or similar for cow's eyes
Polyester toy stuffing or wadding
Yarn needle

## TENSION (GAUGE)
12 sts and 9 rnds to 5cm (2in) using 5.00mm (H-8) hook and yarn MC over dc/sc.

## NOTE
Before beginning the first round in each section, place a marker or short length of contrasting yarn across your crochet and up against the loop on the hook and above the working yarn. Work Rnd 2, then slip the marker out and place it at the beginning of the next round and so on. The marker will indicate where each subsequent round starts.

# Cow

## HEAD & BODY
Using yarn B, beg at the nose end, make 3ch.
**Foundation rnd:** Working over tail end, 8dc/8sc in third ch from hook, join to top of 3ch with sl st to form ring (8dc/8sc).
**Rnd 1:** 1dc/1sc in each of next 8dc/8sc.
**Rnd 2:** 2dc/2sc in each of next 8dc/8sc (16dc/16sc).
**Rnd 3:** 1dc/1sc in each of next 16dc/16sc.

Rep last rnd 3 times more, ending with sl st in top of last dc/sc of rnd.

**Rnd 7:** Join in yarn A to same place as sl st was worked, 1dc/1sc in each of next 16dc/16sc.

**Rnd 8:** 1dc/1sc in each of next 16dc/16sc.
Rep last rnd 5 times more, ending with sl st in top of first dc/sc.

Fasten off, leaving the marker in the crochet so that you can pick up from there after sewing on face markings.

**Add on face markings:**

Using yarn MC, make 24ch, leaving a long tail end for sewing.
Fasten off.

To sew on the face, thread up one end and secure it at the back of the cow's head. Curl the chain into a circular shape that resembles the shape in the photograph, catching chain every so often to secure in place.

Referring to the photograph, sew on the nostrils with black yarn, working a couple of straight stitches for each nostril.

**Cont with the body:**

Rejoin yarn A to sl st at end of last rnd on main body.

**Shape neck:**

**Rnd 14:** *1dc/1sc in each of next 3dc/3sc, miss next dc/sc, rep from * around (12dc/12sc).

**Rnd 15:** 1dc/1sc in each of next 12dc/12sc.

**Rnd 16:** *1dc/1sc in next dc/sc, 2dc/2sc in next, rep from * around (18dc/18sc).
Rep last rnd once more (27dc/27sc).

**Rnd 18:** 1dc/1sc in each of next 27dc/27sc.
Rep last rnd once more.

**Shape belly:**

**Rnd 20:** [1dc/1sc in each of next 2dc/2sc, 2dc/2sc in next dc/sc] twice, 1dc/1sc in each of next 15dc/15sc, [1dc/1sc in each of next 2dc/2sc, 2dc/2sc in next dc/sc] twice (31dc/31sc).

**Rnd 21:** 1dc/1sc in each of next 31dc/31sc.
Rep last rnd 16 times more, ending with sl st in top of first dc/sc.

Fasten off, leaving the marker in the crochet so that you can pick up from there after sewing on body markings.

**Add on body markings:**

Using yarn MC, make 50ch, leaving a long loose end for sewing with. Fasten off.
To sew on the body markings, thread up one end and secure it at the back of the cow's body, near the back end.
Curl the chain into a shape that resembles the shape in the photograph, catching chain every so often to secure in place.

Make a second shape with 70ch to sew onto the body near the neck.

**Cont with the body:**
Rejoin yarn A to sl st at end of last rnd on main body.

**Shape bottom:**
**Rnd 38:** *1dc/1sc in each of next 5dc/5sc, miss next dc/sc, rep from * to last dc/sc, miss last dc/sc (25dc/25sc).
**Rnd 39:** *1dc/1sc in each of next 4dc/4sc, miss next dc/sc, rep from * around (20dc/20sc).
**Rnd 40:** *1dc/1sc in each of next 3dc/3sc, miss next dc/sc, rep from * around (15dc/15sc).
Stuff the cow through the bottom.
**Rnd 41:** *1dc/1sc in each of next 2dc/2sc, miss next dc/sc, rep from * around (10dc/10sc).
**Rnd 42:** *1dc/1sc in next dc/sc, miss next dc/sc, rep from * around until ring is closed.
Fasten off.

## TAIL
Using yarn A, make 7ch, join in yarn MC and make 9ch. Fasten off, weaving in the yarn – leave the black tail end for sewing onto the body.
Using yarn MC, make a fringed end at the back (see instructions on page 93).

## EARS (make 2)
Using yarn A, make 16ch.
**Row 1:** 1dc/1sc in second ch from hook, 1dc/1sc in each ch across (15dc/15sc).
Fasten off yarn A, join in yarn B.
**Row 2:** 1dc/1sc in each of next 15dc/15sc.
Fasten off.

## HORNS (make 2)
Using yarn MC, make 4ch.
**Row 1:** 1dc/1sc in third ch from hook, 1dc/1sc in next ch.
Fasten off, leaving the tail ends for sewing onto the head.

## BLACK LEGS (make 3)
Beg with the hoof, using yarn A, make 3ch.
**Foundation chain:** Working over tail end, 8dc/8sc in third ch from hook (8dc/8sc).
**Rnd 1:** 1dc/1sc in each of next 8dc/8sc.
**Shape sides of hoof:**
Rep last rnd twice more.
**Shape leg:**
**Rnd 4:** *1dc/1sc in each of next 3dc/3sc, miss next dc/sc, rep from * once more (6dc/6sc).
**Rnd 5:** 1dc/1sc in each of next 6dc/6sc.**
Rep last rnd until leg measures 10cm (4in) from hoof.

Fasten off, leaving the tail ends for sewing onto the body.

## BLACK & WHITE LEG

Work as for black leg up to **.

**Rnd 6:** Join in yarn MC, 1dc/1sc in each of next 2dc/2sc, change to yarn A to complete rnd.

**Rnd 7:** In yarn MC, 1dc/1sc in each of next 3dc/3sc, change to yarn A to complete rnd.

**Rnd 8:** In yarn MC, 1dc/1sc in each of next 4dc/4sc, change to yarn A to complete rnd.

**Rnd 9:** In yarn MC, 1dc/1sc in each of next 5dc/5sc, change to yarn A to complete rnd.

Fasten off yarn A.

**Rnd 10:** In yarn MC, 1dc/1sc in each of next 6dc/6sc.

Rep last rnd until leg measures 10cm (4in) from hoof.

Fasten off, leaving the tail ends for sewing onto the body.

## UDDER

**Foundation row:** Using yarn B, make 2ch.

**Rnd 1:** 10dc/10sc in 2nd ch from hook (10dc/10sc).

**Rnd 2:** 2dc/2sc in each dc/sc around (20dc/20sc).

**Rnd 3:** 1dc/1sc in each dc/sc around.

Rep last rnd 3 times more.

Fasten off, pull up the loose end at the start to close the ring.

For the teats, cut four lengths of yarn B 10cm (4in) long. Secure the ends to the inside of the udder, thread through to the front at the foundation row, and let the threads dangle on the right side. Trim them to 1cm (⅜in) from udder.

## TO FINISH

Stuff the legs lightly. Using a blunt-ended yarn needle and MC yarn, sew the four legs to the underside of the body equidistant from each other.

Sew each ear together, bending in half widthways, and joining the pink finishing row. Sew the base of each ear in place, referring to the photograph for accurate positioning.

Sew the widest end of the horns to the top of the head in between the ears.

Sew on a glass bead at either side of the head for the eyes.

Sew the udder to the underside of

the cow, about 2.5cm (1in) away from the bottom, stuffing it a little before completing the sewing. Sew the cow's tail to its bottom.

# Calf

## HEAD & BODY

**Foundation chain:** Using yarn MC and beg at the tail end, make 9ch, join with sl st in first ch to form a ring, taking care not to twist the loop.

**Rnd 1:** 1dc/1sc in each of next 9ch (9dc/9sc).

**Rnd 2:** *1dc/1sc in each of next 2ch, 2dc/2sc in next dc/sc, rep from * around (12dc/12sc).

**Rnd 3:** *1dc/1sc in each of next 3dc/3sc, 2dc/2sc in next dc/sc, rep from * around (15dc/15sc).

Tie yarn A to working yarn, and work it with yarn MC along the back of the work until it is needed.

**Rnd 4:** In MC 1dc/1sc in each of next 4dc/4sc, in yarn A 1dc/1sc in each of next 2dc/2sc, in MC 1dc/1sc in each of next 9dc/9sc.

**Rnd 5:** In MC 1dc/1sc in each of next 2dc/2sc, in yarn A 1dc/1sc in each of next 6dc/6sc, in MC 1dc/1sc in each of next 7dc/7sc.

**Rnd 6:** In MC 1dc/1sc in next dc/sc, in yarn A 1dc/1sc in each of next 8dc/8sc, in MC 1dc/1sc in each of next 6dc/6sc.

**Rnd 7:** In MC 1dc/1sc in each of next 2dc/2sc, in yarn A 1dc/1sc in each of next 6dc/6sc, in MC 1dc/1sc in each of next 7dc/7sc.

**Rnd 8:** In MC 1dc/1sc in each of next 4dc/4sc, in yarn A 1dc/1sc in each of next 2dc/2sc, in MC 1dc/1sc in each of next 9dc/9sc.

Break off yarn A and weave it into the back of the work, cont in yarn MC only.

**Rnd 9:** 1dc/1sc in each of next 15dc/15sc. Rep last rnd 3 times more.

**Shape head:**

**Rnd 13:** *1dc/1sc in each of next 2dc/2sc, miss next dc/sc, rep from * around (10dc/10sc).

**Rnd 14:** 1dc/1sc in each dc/sc around.

**Rnd 15:** *1dc/1sc in next dc/sc, miss next dc/sc, rep from * around (5dc/5sc).

**Rnd 16:** 1dc/1sc in each dc/sc around. Rep last rnd 5 times more.

**Rnd 22:** *1dc/1sc in next dc/sc, miss next dc/sc, rep from * around, rep until ring closes.

Fasten off, weave in end.

For the pink disc at the end of the nose, using yarn B, make 2ch, 7dc/7sc in

2nd ch from hook, ending sl st in top of first dc/sc.
Fasten off.

## EARS (make 2)
**Foundation chain:** Using yarn MC, make 6ch, fasten off.

## TAIL
**Foundation chain:** Using yarn MC, make 10ch, fasten off.
Make a fringed end with 3 lengths of yarn, trimmed to 12mm (½in) afterwards (see instructions on page 93).

## LEGS (make 4)
**Foundation chain:** Using yarn MC, make 9ch.

**Row 1:** 1dc/1sc in second ch from hook, 1dc/1sc in each ch across, turn (8dc/8sc).
**Row 2:** 1ch, 1dc/1sc in each dc/sc across, turn.
Fasten off.

## TO FINISH
Sew up the seam at the back of the legs, then, with yarn A, sew on a couple of straight stitches at each side of the foot for hooves. With your finger in the puppet, taking care not to pinch yourself, sew on the two ears joining both ends. Sew on two eyes, stitching a French knot for each with the black yarn. Sew the pink disk to the end of the nose. Sew on the tail and the legs.

## Acknowledgements

I would like to extend a huge thank you to Michelle Lo and Katie Cowan for inviting me to do this book, and for lighting my creative flair!

Also, a huge thank you to the wonderful team at Collins & Brown, in particular Gemma Wilson, Ben, Ruth, Mark Winwood for his ability to make toys come to life, Amy, Komal, Joanna and Laura. A special big cheer for kindly Katie Hudson, with her gentle liaising and infectious enthusiasm.

It was really great to work with you all.

### Picture credits
Cover photography by Rachel Whiting
Photography by Mark Winwood